Anxious Attachment

How to Regulate & Self Soothe Your Emotions, Build Intimate Relationships and Overcome Relationship Anxiety

Rose Novak

Table of Content

Introduction

Marilyn's Story: The Struggle of Pushing Others Away

With shaky hands gripping her coffee mug, Marilyn sat opposite her friend in the dimly lit café. Tears welled up as she recounted her history of unsatisfying relationships that left her feeling broken and unworthy. "I just don't understand why I keep driving people away," she whispered, her voice trembling.

The Vicious Cycle of Love and Self-Sabotage

Do you find yourself longing for love, yet somehow sabotaging every relationship? Like Marilyn, you're not alone. Navigating attachment styles, particularly anxious attachment, can feel like a relentless battle, full of insecurity, fear of rejection, and an overwhelming need for approval.

The Roots of Attachment Theory: An Emotional Journey

Imagine a small child, devastated and clinging to their parent as they leave for work. This poignant image embodies the essence of attachment theory, a framework that explores how early experiences shape our emotional development. Understanding attachment isn't just about academic theory; it's about uncovering the deep emotional patterns that shape how we relate to others, view ourselves, and form intimate bonds.

Why Knowing Your Attachment Style is Crucial

Whether your attachment style leads you to anxiously seek validation or withdraw in fear of rejection, recognizing your tendencies is essential for healing and personal growth. It's time to understand how your attachment style influences your self-esteem, relationships, and overall well-being.

A Journey Toward Healing and Self-Discovery

For too long, individuals with anxious attachment have been dismissed as "needy" or "insecure," left to battle their inner turmoil alone. But what if there was a roadmap to guide you from your painful past to a brighter, safer future? That's the purpose of this book—to help illuminate your path toward recovery and self-awareness.

This book offers life-changing insights into how to overcome the struggles that prevent you from enjoying fulfilling relationships. If you've ever felt uneasy in relationships, struggled to balance intimacy with independence, or found it hard to set boundaries, you've come to the right place. Through these pages, you will find practical strategies and powerful insights to help you navigate your relationships with clarity and confidence.

Common Challenges and How This Book Can Help

Let's delve into some of the specific issues you might face and how this book offers solutions:

1. **Fear of Abandonment:** One of the most paralyzing struggles is the fear of abandonment. Constant worry that your partner might leave can hinder your ability to thrive. Don't worry; this book provides actionable tools to overcome your fears and build a sense of security. Activities and reflective practices will help you develop courage and trust in your relationships.
2. **Seeking Validation from Others:** Your worth should never be dictated by others. This book introduces powerful strategies to break the cycle of relying on external approval. You'll discover practical ways to foster internal self-esteem, helping you recognize your value without needing validation from others.
3. **Struggling to Trust Others:** Trust is fundamental, yet it can be one of the hardest things to cultivate. You'll find helpful guidance here on how to rebuild trust and open up in relationships. Through empathy-building exercises, you will learn how to approach trust issues with grace and persistence.
4. **Emotional Sensitivity:** Sensitivity can be both a gift and a challenge. Misunderstood, it often leads to pain, but when managed well, it enhances emotional connections. This book will help you harness the power of your emotions through mindfulness and emotional management techniques, turning sensitivity into a source of strength.
5. **Balancing Intimacy and Independence:** Struggling to find a balance between closeness and personal space? This

common challenge can be resolved. You'll learn methods to respect both your need for connection and your desire for independence, creating a healthier balance in your relationships through self-reflection and communication exercises.

6. **Setting Boundaries:** For some, setting boundaries feels impossible. Boundaries are essential for personal well-being and relationship health. This book provides step-by-step advice on how to set and maintain healthy boundaries without guilt, using real-life examples and practical strategies.

7. **Overanalyzing the Relationship:** Constantly overthinking every word and gesture is exhausting. This book will help you break free from the cycle of over-analysis. Through cognitive-behavioral techniques and mindfulness practices, you'll learn how to quiet your mind and engage more authentically with your partner.

8. **Fear of Expressing Your Needs:** Your needs matter. This book offers practical exercises to overcome the fear of expressing them. With role-playing and communication techniques, you'll gain the confidence to voice your needs clearly, fostering deeper understanding and connection in your relationship.

Are You Ready to Transform Your Relationships?: Are you seeking a credible, evidence-based guide on managing anxious attachment in relationships? Look no further than Rose Novak's insightful work. With a master's degree in psychology and years of experience leading workshops and group therapy, Novak's practical approach sets her apart. Dive into her book and begin your journey to emotional wellness and secure, loving relationships.

Rose's personal journey makes her incredibly relatable to readers dealing with similar struggles. Her deep passion for understanding emotions and relationships shines through in her dedication to helping others navigate toward healthier attachments and personal growth. Not to mention, she's also an avid lover of nature, a literature enthusiast, and a photography aficionado! This well-rounded perspective adds an extra layer of authenticity and empathy to her writing. With her expertise, practical experience, and heartfelt insights, Rose Novak stands out as a trustworthy authority on attachment styles and relationships—you won't be disappointed!

A Deeper Understanding of Yourself and Your Relationships

By delving into attachment styles and their impact on behavior, this book offers a powerful tool for self-discovery. You'll gain profound clarity on your emotional needs and how these affect your relationships. With a focus on anxious attachment, Rose uses the latest research in neuroscience, mindfulness, and psychology to provide actionable strategies that will help you break free from old patterns and find the love and emotional fulfillment you seek. Each chapter is filled with practical solutions and life-changing insights to help you tackle these challenges head-on.

Transform Your Relationships with Practical Insights

But there's even more! This book equips you with the tools to confidently manage all your relationships. From learning effective communication skills to setting healthy boundaries and building trust and intimacy, you'll discover how to foster more fulfilling, harmonious connections with your partners. By understanding both your own attachment style and your partner's, you'll be able to cultivate deeper intimacy and a stronger emotional bond, enhancing closeness, trust, and mutual understanding.

Personal Growth and Empowerment Await

The best part? By shedding limiting patterns, embracing your true self, and pursuing meaningful relationships aligned with your values, you'll experience a profound sense of empowerment and personal growth. As you address the fears and insecurities tied to attachment, you'll feel less anxiety and stress in your relationships, allowing you to enjoy a greater sense of peace, security, and emotional well-being.

Ready for Positive Change?

So, what are you waiting for? If you're eager to learn more about yourself and your relationships, turn the page and get ready for a positive transformation in your life!

Chapter 1:
Grasping the Basics of Attachment Theory

One of the most powerful frameworks for understanding the intricacies of human relationships is attachment theory. Originally proposed by psychologist John Bowlby in the mid-20th century, this theory suggests that the bonds formed between infants and their primary caregivers set the stage for future emotional and relational experiences.

Imagine an infant curled up in their mother's arms, seeking warmth and security.

This deep-seated need for connection is not a fleeting desire; it establishes a lifelong path of attachment that influences how we relate to others and ourselves. Attachment theory revolves around the idea of a "secure base"—a sense of safety we return to when faced with emotional distress. When caregivers respond to a child's needs with consistency and compassion, they foster trust and resilience, laying the groundwork for secure attachment. However, this is not everyone's experience. For some, childhoods marked by trauma, neglect, or inconsistent care lead to insecure attachment patterns.

Understanding how these early bonds shape our emotional lives is key to grasping attachment theory. It goes beyond simply analyzing infant-caregiver interactions; it offers a comprehensive model for exploring self-regulation, emotional resilience, and the capacity to form close relationships. In the following sections, we will delve into the intricacies of attachment styles, revealing their nuances and unlocking new possibilities for growth. Together, we will explore how these connections impact our relationships and uncover the mysteries of human attachment.

Attachment Styles: Secure, Anxious, and Avoidant

Our early relationships with caregivers heavily influence our attachment styles, which, in turn, shape how we navigate connections throughout life. These patterns—secure, anxious, and avoidant—help explain our approach to intimacy, emotional expression, and conflict resolution.

- **Secure Attachment:** People with secure attachment feel confident and safe in their relationships. They are comfortable expressing their needs, offering support to their partners, and addressing conflicts with honesty and understanding. They maintain a balanced and positive view of themselves and their relationships.
- **Anxious Attachment:** Those with anxious attachment crave constant validation and are often highly sensitive to the threat of rejection. Their relationships may be marked by intense fluctuations between clinginess and withdrawal, and they often struggle with self-worth, seeking others' approval to feel secure.
- **Avoidant Attachment:** Individuals with avoidant attachment prioritize independence over intimacy and tend to avoid relying on others. They keep their emotional distance, finding it challenging to open up or form deep connections, often as a way to protect themselves from vulnerability and rejection.

The goal of understanding attachment styles isn't to place blame but to recognize the patterns that influence our relationships. By gaining insight into these behaviors, we can build healthier, more meaningful connections. As we continue through this book, we'll break down each attachment style in detail, providing the tools necessary to deepen your self-awareness and improve your relationships.

The Development of Attachment Styles

Attachment styles begin forming in infancy, shaped by a blend of psychological, biological, and environmental factors. Early interactions with caregivers are crucial in developing these patterns, which later influence how we approach relationships in adulthood.

Infants are naturally inclined to seek comfort and closeness from their caregivers, as this provides a sense of security and enhances survival. Through social referencing, babies learn to interpret their caregivers' signals, which helps them build strong attachment bonds.

During the first year of life, caregivers play a critical role in shaping attachment styles by consistently responding to an infant's needs. Reliable and sensitive caregiving leads to secure attachment, fostering trust in the child's ability to rely on others for support.

Conversely, inconsistent or neglectful caregiving can result in insecure attachment patterns. Anxious attachment may develop when caregivers are unpredictable, causing children to become hyper-aware of potential abandonment. Avoidant attachment often stems from emotional unavailability, teaching the child to self-soothe and rely less on others.

As children grow, their attachment styles continue to evolve through relationships with caregivers, friends, and romantic partners. These early patterns significantly influence how we experience intimacy, navigate interactions, and handle conflict in adult relationships.

Although attachment styles tend to remain consistent, they are not fixed. With increased self-awareness and therapeutic support, individuals can cultivate more secure attachment patterns, leading to more fulfilling relationships. Understanding how these styles develop is vital to unraveling the complexities of human relationships, fostering empathy, and enhancing emotional connections with ourselves and others.

Key Insights:

- **Early Beginnings:** Attachment theory suggests that our earliest interactions with caregivers shape our attachment styles and impact how we engage in relationships throughout life.
- **Three Main Styles:** The chapter highlights the three primary attachment styles—secure, anxious, and avoidant— each with distinct behavioral and emotional patterns in relationships.
- **Adult Relationship Impact:** Recognizing your attachment style provides valuable insight into how you communicate, handle emotions, and resolve conflicts in relationships.
- **Childhood's Role:** Parental responsiveness and emotional availability play a pivotal role in shaping attachment styles and influence adult relationships.

- **Room for Change:** Although attachment styles are generally stable, they are not permanent. With self-awareness and deliberate effort, individuals can move toward a more secure attachment style and nurture healthier relationships.
- **The Value of Secure Attachment:** Secure attachment fosters trust, intimacy, and mutual support, serving as the foundation for healthy, lasting relationships.

Action Steps:

- Reflect on your attachment style and consider how it has influenced your relationships.
- Contemplate how your childhood experiences may have shaped your attachment patterns.

Stay tuned for the next chapter, where we will explore how to recognize and shift your attachment style to foster healthier, more fulfilling relationships.

Chapter 2:

Understanding the Anxious Attachment Style

Individuals with an anxious attachment style often exhibit certain behaviors and thought patterns driven by underlying fears and insecurities in their relationships. These tendencies frequently trace back to childhood experiences of inconsistent caregiving or a perceived threat of abandonment, which results in heightened sensitivity to rejection. Below are key traits typically associated with anxious attachment:

1. **Fixation on Relationships**

   Those with anxious attachment tend to place a significant emphasis on relationships, devoting substantial time and effort to maintaining emotional connections. They often seek constant reassurance and validation from their partners, fearing that any sign of distance or conflict might lead to abandonment.

2. **Fear of Abandonment**

   A strong fear of rejection or being left behind is common among individuals with anxious attachment. This fear may manifest in behaviors like being overly clingy, possessive, or jealous. Even minor setbacks or perceived slights can be viewed as indicators of impending rejection, which leads to increased anxiety and emotional turmoil.

3. **Heightened Sensitivity to Rejection**

   People with anxious attachment are highly attuned to any signs of disapproval or rejection. They may interpret even small, inconsistent actions from their partner as warning signals of abandonment. Constantly monitoring their partner's emotions and behaviors, they often seek validation of their worth and desirability.

4. **Seeking Constant Reassurance and Validation**

To alleviate their fear of abandonment, individuals with anxious attachment frequently seek reassurance and validation from their partners. They may constantly look for confirmation of their worth or physical appeal, leading to behaviors such as needing frequent validation or experiencing emotional outbursts when reassurance is not immediately available.

5. **Emotional Intensity**

People with anxious attachment often experience heightened emotions, frequently oscillating between extremes of love and fear in their relationships. Intense feelings of insecurity or fear of rejection can trigger emotional outbursts or attempts to manipulate their partner's behavior to gain validation.

6. **Trust Issues**

Trusting others can be difficult for those with anxious attachment, largely due to past experiences of inconsistent caregiving or betrayal. They may idolize their partners one moment, only to be consumed by the fear of being abandoned the next, resulting in a state of emotional instability and unpredictability.

7. **Dependence on External Validation**

Individuals with anxious attachment often base their self-worth on external validation, particularly in the context of their relationships. They may prioritize their partner's approval over their own needs and desires, sacrificing independence and well-being in the pursuit of reassurance.

By understanding these common traits, individuals with anxious attachment can start recognizing patterns in their behavior and take steps toward healthier emotional regulation and more balanced relationships.

four main attachment styles, categorized by two primary dimensions: the **model of self** (positive or negative) and the **model of others** (positive or negative). These dimensions also align with **levels of anxiety** (high or low) and **avoidance** (high or low).

Here's a breakdown of the attachment styles in the diagram:

1. **Secure Attachment**
   o **Model of Self**: Positive (Low Anxiety)
   o **Model of Others**: Positive (Low Avoidance)
   o **Traits**: Confidence, resilience, and reciprocity in relationships. Individuals are non-reactive and comfortable with closeness.
2. **Anxious Attachment**
   o **Model of Self**: Negative (High Anxiety)
   o **Model of Others**: Positive (Low Avoidance)
   o **Traits**: Emotional hunger, fantasy bonds, turbulence in relationships, and a lack of nurturing. Individuals are constantly seeking reassurance from others.
3. **Avoidant Attachment**
   o **Model of Self**: Positive (Low Anxiety)
   o **Model of Others**: Negative (High Avoidance)
   o **Traits**: Emotional distance, ambivalence, isolation, and ambiguity in relationships. These individuals tend to avoid intimacy and connection.
4. **Fearful Attachment**
   o **Model of Self**: Negative (High Anxiety)
   o **Model of Others**: Negative (High Avoidance)
   o **Traits**: Unpredictability, disorganization, internal conflict, and dramatic responses. These individuals often experience confusion about closeness and distance in relationships.

This visual guide provides a clear overview of how early experiences and internalized beliefs about oneself and others contribute to the development of these attachment styles, which affect adult relational behaviors.

Gaining insight into the characteristics of anxious attachment can provide a deeper understanding of the underlying causes of insecurity in relationships, paving the way for healing and personal growth. By recognizing and addressing these patterns, individuals can cultivate self-awareness, emotional resilience, and a greater sense of security in their relationships, ultimately leading to deeper intimacy and emotional fulfillment.

Origins and Causes of Anxious Attachment

Anxious attachment often forms during childhood when attachment patterns are established, influenced by a variety of factors. These include:

1. **Inconsistent Caregiver Responsiveness**

   One of the most common causes of anxious attachment is unpredictable or inconsistent caregiving during infancy. When caregivers are sometimes attentive and nurturing but at other times emotionally distant or unresponsive, infants develop attachment insecurities. This inconsistency can lead to confusion and anxiety in the child, who becomes unsure when or if their emotional needs will be met.

2. **Childhood Trauma or Separation**

   Traumatic events such as parental divorce, the death of a caregiver, or extended separations during infancy can severely impact a child's ability to form secure attachments. These experiences can embed a deep sense of vulnerability and insecurity, which may manifest as a fear of abandonment in later relationships.

3. **Influence of Parental Attachment Styles**

   A caregiver's own attachment style plays a critical role in shaping the attachment patterns of their children. Parents with insecure attachment styles, such as anxious or avoidant attachment, may struggle to provide consistent emotional validation and support. This can perpetuate a cycle of insecurity, with children inheriting their parents' attachment anxieties.

4. **Family Dynamics and Dysfunction**

   Dysfunctional family environments, such as those marked by frequent conflict, emotional abuse, or enmeshment, can contribute to the development of anxious attachment. Children raised in such unstable or chaotic households may become hypervigilant and anxious, always on edge, fearing emotional abandonment in their future relationships.

5. **Temperamental Factors**

Some individuals may be more predisposed to anxious attachment due to inherent temperament traits, such as heightened sensitivity to stress or emotional instability. When combined with inconsistent caregiving, these temperamental factors can exacerbate fears of rejection and abandonment, making relationships particularly fraught for those who are naturally more anxious or sensitive.

6. **Cultural and Social Influences**

Cultural norms and societal views on attachment and relationships can also shape attachment styles. In cultures that emphasize emotional restraint and self-reliance, individuals may feel shame or inadequacy when expressing their need for connection, which can heighten feelings of anxiety and insecurity in relationships.

7. **Impact on Adult Relationships**

Anxious attachment formed in childhood often has lasting effects, influencing a person's intimate relationships and social interactions well into adulthood. Individuals with anxious attachment may repeatedly find themselves drawn to partners who exhibit similar patterns of emotional inconsistency or unavailability, perpetuating a cycle of unhealthy relationship dynamics.

Path to Healing and Growth

While the impact of anxious attachment can be significant, understanding its origins offers a crucial first step toward breaking unhealthy patterns and fostering personal growth. With increased self-awareness, therapeutic support, and nurturing relationships, individuals can overcome the challenges of anxious attachment and develop more secure and fulfilling relationships.

By identifying and addressing these patterns, individuals can rewrite their relational narratives, building stronger emotional connections and experiencing deeper security in their relationships. Through mindful effort, healing from anxious attachment is not only possible but also transformative, leading to more meaningful and rewarding interpersonal experiences.

The Impact of Anxious Attachment on Relationships and Mental Health

Anxious attachment can have a significant impact on both relationships and mental well-being, affecting many aspects of a person's emotional life. Understanding these effects is crucial for personal growth and healing.

How Anxious Attachment Affects Relationships

1. **Communication Challenges**

   Individuals with anxious attachment often struggle with effective communication. Their constant need for reassurance and fear of abandonment may make it difficult for them to clearly express their needs and set boundaries. This can lead to misunderstandings and frustration within the relationship.

2. **Issues with Intimacy**

   Emotional closeness can become a challenge for people with anxious attachment. Fear of rejection or engulfment may cause them to either cling too tightly to their partner or mentally withdraw, making it difficult to build vulnerability and deeper emotional connections.

3. **Trust Problems**

   Trust is often a significant issue for people with anxious attachment due to past experiences of abandonment or betrayal. They may constantly second-guess their partner's intentions, leading to insecurity, jealousy, and feelings of inadequacy.

4. **Dependency and Codependency**

Individuals with anxious attachment often rely heavily on their partner for emotional validation and self-worth, sacrificing their independence and sense of self in the process. This imbalance can create unhealthy dynamics and lead to codependency within relationships.

5. Cycle of Rejection and Reassurance

A constant cycle of seeking reassurance followed by fears of rejection is common in anxious attachment. This emotional rollercoaster can create instability in the relationship, leading to frustration, resentment, and ongoing conflicts.

How Anxious Attachment Affects Mental Health

1. Stress and Anxiety

Individuals with anxious attachment often experience elevated levels of stress and anxiety within relationships. Persistent fears of rejection or abandonment may manifest physically, with symptoms such as increased heart rate, muscle tension, and insomnia.

2. Low Self-Esteem

A core issue for those with anxious attachment is weak self-esteem. They may constantly feel that they are not good enough or unworthy of love, reinforcing negative self-perceptions and fostering feelings of inadequacy.

3. Depression

Prolonged feelings of rejection and loneliness in relationships can contribute to symptoms of depression. A sense of hopelessness or despair may grow when individuals struggle to establish meaningful, lasting connections.

4. Difficulty Adapting to Change

People with anxious attachment often find it challenging to cope with changes or disruptions in their relationships. Fear that any deviation from their expectations will lead to rejection or loss can increase anxiety and strain the relationship further.

5. **Overall Health Impact**

   The emotional toll of anxious attachment extends beyond relationships, impacting a person's overall well-being and quality of life. Chronic feelings of insecurity, loneliness, and sadness can hinder personal growth, confidence, and fulfillment in many aspects of life.

Path to Healing and Growth

Recognizing the impact of anxious attachment on relationships and mental health is the first step toward healing and personal development. By cultivating self-awareness, engaging in therapy, and building supportive relationships, individuals can begin to break free from unhealthy attachment patterns and create more secure, fulfilling connections.

Key Takeaways:

- **Characteristics of Anxious Attachment**: Those with anxious attachment often crave closeness and reassurance but may experience significant anxiety about their partner's availability and commitment.
- **Origins in Childhood**: Anxious attachment typically stems from inconsistent caregiving in childhood, leading to a fear of abandonment and a need for validation.
- **Behavioral Patterns**: People with anxious attachment may exhibit clinginess, a constant need for reassurance, and difficulty with trust.
- **Relationship Impact**: Anxious attachment often leads to jealousy, dependency, and emotional instability in relationships, causing conflict and insecurity.
- **Breaking the Cycle**: Self-awareness and self-soothing strategies are essential for managing anxiety and creating healthier relationship patterns.
- **Communication Strategies**: Effective communication helps anxious individuals express their needs and fears constructively, fostering deeper intimacy and understanding.

- **Building Security**: Developing self-reliance and challenging negative beliefs can help individuals transition toward a more secure attachment style, promoting greater self-esteem and healthier relationships.

Action Steps:

- Reflect on how the traits of anxious attachment resonate with your own relationship experiences.
- Identify specific behaviors or thought patterns you exhibit that may stem from an anxious attachment style.

Stay tuned for the next chapter, where we will explore practical strategies to transform anxious attachment patterns and build greater security and fulfillment in relationships.

Chapter 3:
Identifying Anxious Attachment Patterns

Our attachment styles are deeply intertwined with our early life experiences, shaped by the relationships and environments we were exposed to as children. Understanding the origin of your attachment style requires an exploration of your childhood, where the interactions and emotional exchanges with caregivers played a foundational role in how you connect with others today.

When we are born, we possess an inherent need to seek proximity and connection with our caregivers. These figures, often our parents or primary caregivers, provide essential comfort, security, and support. The consistency and quality of these early relationships significantly influence the development of our attachment style.

For individuals with a **secure attachment style**, early experiences of stable, consistent caregiving create a strong foundation for healthy relationship dynamics. Securely attached individuals develop trust in their caregivers' availability and responsiveness, fostering a sense of confidence and security in their relationships.

In contrast, **insecure attachment styles**—such as anxious or avoidant—can arise from early experiences of inconsistency, neglect, or trauma. Anxious attachment typically develops when caregivers are unpredictable in their availability or responsiveness, causing heightened anxiety and a fear of abandonment in the child. On the other hand, avoidant attachment may emerge when caregivers are emotionally distant or dismissive, prompting the child to minimize dependence on others and learn to self-soothe.

To trace the roots of your attachment style, it is essential to reflect on the patterns of emotional regulation, communication, and interaction that characterized your early relationships. You can uncover the messages you internalized about love, intimacy, and worthiness, and how these beliefs continue to impact your behavior and relationship dynamics as an adult.

Through self-reflection, therapy, and supportive relationships, it is possible to unpack these early experiences with curiosity and compassion. By doing so, you can gain greater awareness of your attachment patterns and take steps toward healing, growth, and fostering healthier, more satisfying relationships in the present and future.

Self-Assessment Exercises to Explore Your Attachment Style

Engaging in self-assessment exercises is a valuable way to gain insights into your attachment style and relational patterns. Here are several exercises to help you reflect and build self-awareness:

1. **Reflect on Your Early Relationships**

   Take some time to think about your early relationships with caregivers, family members, and peers. How responsive and supportive were these figures? Reflect on how the quality of these interactions may have influenced your attachment style and emotional responses today.

2. **Identify Patterns in Your Current Relationships**

   Observe recurring themes in your current relationships, whether they are romantic partnerships, friendships, or even professional interactions. Do you notice fears of abandonment, challenges with trust, or a reliance on external validation? Reflect on how these patterns might be tied to your attachment style.

3. **Explore Your Emotional Responses**

   Pay attention to your emotional reactions, especially in situations involving intimacy, vulnerability, or conflict. Are your emotions intense or difficult to manage? Do you tend to feel anxious or avoidant in certain situations? Exploring these responses can offer insights into how your attachment style affects your emotional regulation.

4. **Consider Your Relationship History**

Review your past relationships—both the positive and challenging ones. Reflect on how your attachment style may have influenced your approach to intimacy, communication, and conflict resolution. What patterns do you recognize in your relationship history?

5. **Assess Your Self-Worth and Security**

Reflect on your sense of self-worth and security in your relationships. Do you often seek validation or approval from others? Do you struggle with feelings of inadequacy? These beliefs may be linked to your attachment style, and recognizing them can help you address them constructively.

6. **Seek Feedback from Trusted Others**

Ask trusted friends, family members, or mental health professionals for feedback on your attachment style and relational behaviors. Their insights may offer valuable perspectives on how you interact in relationships and areas where you might want to grow.

7. **Engage in Self-Reflection and Journaling**

Dedicate time to self-reflection and journaling to explore your thoughts and feelings related to attachment. Writing about your insights, challenges, and emotional responses can help clarify your attachment patterns and guide you toward personal growth.

The Importance of Patience and Compassion in Self-Assessment

Remember that self-assessment is a gradual, ongoing process. It is important to approach these exercises with patience and self-compassion. You are not expected to have all the answers immediately, and it's okay to take your time as you explore these reflections.

By engaging in these exercises, you can gain deeper insight into your attachment style and lay the foundation for personal growth, healing, and the creation of more fulfilling relationships. This self-awareness can empower you to break free from old patterns and cultivate healthier, more secure connections with others.

Exercises for Exploring Attachment Styles

Here's a summary of the key signs:

1. **Constant Need for Reassurance**: Continuously seeking affirmation from their partner, such as asking "Do you love me?" or other forms of validation to feel secure.
2. **Worry of Rejection**: Persistent thoughts like "He's going to dump me," reflecting a constant fear of being abandoned or rejected by their partner.
3. **Fear of Infidelity**: Anxiety about their partner's loyalty, shown by suspicion over who their partner is communicating with, such as "Who's texting him?"
4. **Consuming Fixation on the Relationship**: Focusing excessively on the relationship, often to the exclusion of other aspects of life, as depicted by thoughts like "You're what matters."
5. **Panic or Jealousy with Distance**: Feeling uneasy or insecure when separated from their partner, frequently checking in, such as asking "How's the trip, hon?"
6. **Frequent Need to Please**: Going out of the way to cater to the partner's needs or asking, "Need anything?" as a way to feel indispensable and maintain the partner's affection.

These behaviors and thoughts often stem from deep-rooted insecurities and fear of abandonment, common in individuals with anxious attachment styles.

Attachment Style Questionnaire

Use this questionnaire to assess your attachment style by reflecting on your behaviors, thoughts, and feelings in relationships. Each statement asks you to consider how much you agree or disagree, helping to identify dimensions such as anxiety, avoidance, and security.

Instructions: Please indicate the extent to which you agree or disagree with each statement.

1. I find it relatively easy to get close to others.
2. I am comfortable depending on others.
3. I worry about being abandoned by those I care about.
4. I often worry that my partner doesn't really love me.
5. I find it difficult to trust others completely.
6. I prefer not to show others how I feel deep down.
7. I often feel uncomfortable when my partner gets too close.
8. I worry that my partner will leave me for someone else.
9. I find it difficult to be alone for long periods.
10. I often worry that I'm not good enough for my partner.
11. I tend to cling to my partner when I feel anxious or insecure.
12. I have a hard time letting go of past hurts in relationships.
13. I often worry that people will reject or criticize me.
14. I feel uncomfortable expressing my needs and desires in relationships.
15. I tend to avoid close relationships because I fear being hurt.
16. I have difficulty trusting others' intentions.
17. I worry that my partner will lose interest in me over time.
18. I often feel anxious or insecure in my relationships.
19. I have a tendency to become overly dependent on my partner.
20. I have a hard time accepting compliments or praise from others.
21. I often worry about being rejected or abandoned by my friends.
22. I tend to feel jealous or possessive in my relationships.
23. I have difficulty expressing my emotions openly and honestly.
24. I find it hard to forgive others for past mistakes or betrayals.
25. I worry that I'm not attractive or desirable enough for my partner.
26. I often feel anxious or insecure when my partner spends time with others.
27. I tend to avoid conflict or confrontation in my relationships.
28. I have difficulty setting boundaries with others in relationships.
29. I often feel misunderstood or unappreciated by my partner.
30. I worry that my partner will find someone better than me.
31. I tend to seek constant reassurance from my partner.
32. I often feel insecure about my worthiness of love and affection.
33. I worry that my partner will become distant or uninterested in me.
34. I find it hard to open up and be vulnerable with others.
35. I tend to idealize romantic partners or relationships.

36. I often feel like I need to earn love or approval from others.
37. I have difficulty expressing my needs and desires in a relationship.
38. I worry that my partner will leave me if I express my true feelings.
39. I feel anxious or insecure when my partner spends time away from me.
40. I often feel like I'm not enough for my partner.
41. I tend to compare myself unfavorably to others in my partner's life.
42. I feel uneasy when my partner spends time with friends or colleagues without me.
43. I often feel like I have to prove my worthiness of love or attention.
44. I tend to seek validation from others to feel good about myself.
45. I worry that my partner will lose interest in me if I'm not perfect.
46. I find it difficult to trust my partner's intentions.
47. I feel anxious or uncomfortable when my partner talks about their past relationships.
48. I often feel like I need to change myself to be worthy of love.
49. I worry that my partner will leave me if I make a mistake.
50. I have a hard time feeling secure in my partner's love and affection.

Note: For each of these items, select the response that best represents your feelings:

- Strongly Agree
- Agree
- Neutral
- Disagree
- Strongly Disagree

After completing the questionnaire, reflect on the patterns you observe in your responses. This self-assessment can help you understand your attachment style and its impact on your relationships.

Relationship Timeline Exercise

Instructions: Reflect on your past relationships and list significant events or milestones for each relationship. Include your emotional responses and note any recurring patterns or behaviors that may have influenced the dynamics of the relationship. This exercise will help you gain insight into your relational patterns and how they have evolved over time.

Timeline of Relationship Events:

1. **2010 - First Date**
   o **Description**: Went to dinner at a fancy restaurant. Had a great conversation and felt a strong connection.
   o **Emotions/Impact**: Excited, nervous, hopeful. Felt like this could be the start of something special.
2. **2011 - Moved in Together**
   o **Description**: Decided to take the next step in the relationship and moved in together. Set up the first apartment and adjusted to living together.
   o **Emotions/Impact**: Happy, excited, but also anxious about sharing space and responsibilities.
3. **2012 - Job Loss**
   o **Description**: Lost a job unexpectedly, causing financial strain and stress in the relationship. Managed through the challenging time together.
   o **Emotions/Impact**: Frustrated, stressed, but grateful for the partner's support.
4. **2013 - Engagement**
   o **Description**: Proposed to the partner during a romantic getaway. Celebrated love and commitment to each other.
   o **Emotions/Impact**: Overjoyed, ecstatic, felt like a dream come true.
5. **2015 - Marriage**
   o **Description**: Tied the knot in a beautiful ceremony surrounded by friends and family. Started the journey as a married couple.
   o **Emotions/Impact**: Blissful, grateful, excited for the future together.

This timeline outlines important relationship events, providing a clear picture of the milestones that shaped the emotional and relational journey of the couple.

Reflection Questions for Relationship Timeline Exercise:

1. **Patterns and Themes**: What consistent patterns or recurring themes do you observe in your relationship timeline? Do certain behaviors or emotions repeat across different relationships or stages?

2. **Impact on Relationship**: How have the significant events and milestones shaped your relationship and the way you perceive each other? Have these events strengthened or strained the relationship?

3. **Unresolved Conflicts**: Are there any conflicts or challenges that remain unresolved? Reflect on how you can address these issues to foster healthier dynamics moving forward.

4. **Self and Partner Awareness**: What insights have you gained about yourself and your partner through this exercise? How have these insights shaped your understanding of your attachment style and relationship needs?

Take time to thoughtfully complete the timeline, and use these reflection questions to deepen your understanding of your relationship dynamics. This exercise can also promote open communication with your partner.

Letter to Your Younger Self

Writing a letter to your younger self can be a powerful way to process and heal past experiences that have shaped your attachment style. Here is a sample of what this letter might look like:

Sample Letter to Your Younger Self

Dear Younger Self,

As I sit down to write this letter, I want to reflect on the journey you've been through. It hasn't always been easy, has it? There were moments of happiness but also times when you felt misunderstood, unloved, or alone. Growing up, our experiences with caregivers and family members shaped so much of who we are today, especially how we view ourselves and the world around us.

I know that at times, you felt insecure and craved validation, always seeking love and approval. But I want you to know that none of this reflected your worth. You were always deserving of love and connection, even when the world didn't make it clear.

Our early experiences may have left lasting impressions, but those experiences do not define us. I see your strength, your resilience, and your ability to cope. You've learned to navigate life in the best way you knew how, and that's something to be proud of.

As we continue to grow, I want to remind you that it's okay to lean on others for support. It's okay to be vulnerable, to ask for help, and to embrace the parts of you that need healing. You are worthy of love, belonging, and happiness, and the future holds so much promise.

Attachment Style Role-Play Exercise

This role-play exercise is designed to help you explore and understand the dynamics of different attachment styles. Engaging in this with a trusted friend or therapist can enhance empathy and communication.

Instructions:

- Find a partner and decide who will play each role: anxious or avoidant attachment.
- Take turns enacting scenarios based on the prompts provided below.
- Reflect on your emotional reactions and how they relate to your real-life attachment style.

Scenarios:

1. **Anxious Attachment Style**

Situation: Your partner has been distant, and you feel worried that they are losing interest

Role-Play: The partner playing the anxious attachment style expresses insecurity by asking, "Are you upset with me?" or "Do you still love me?" The other partner responds according to their attachment style, either offering reassurance or withdrawing.

2. **Avoidant Attachment Style**

Situation: Your partner wants to spend more time together, but you feel overwhelmed and want more space.

Role-Play: The partner playing the avoidant attachment style expresses a need for independence, saying, "I just need some time alone," while the other partner responds with either understanding or frustration.

3. **Conflict Resolution**

Situation: A small disagreement escalates into an argument.

Role-Play: Both partners express their needs and emotions. The anxious partner may seek validation, while the avoidant partner withdraws. Practice resolving the conflict using active listening and empathy.

Reflection Questions:

1. How did it feel to embody a different attachment style?
2. What emotions came up during the role-play?
3. Did any behaviors align with your real-life attachment style?
4. How can you use what you learned to improve communication in your relationships?

Attachment Style Journal Prompts:

Use these prompts to explore your attachment style and relational experiences in depth:

- How do I typically respond to conflict or disagreements in relationships?
- What insecurities arise when I feel emotionally vulnerable?
- How do I seek validation or reassurance from others during distress?
- Reflect on a relationship where you felt particularly secure or insecure. What contributed to those feelings?

Attachment Style Visualization Exercise:

Close your eyes and visualize a moment from your childhood when you felt completely safe and loved. Focus on the emotions, sensations, and memories that arise. This exercise helps you reconnect with feelings of security and stability, promoting inner calm and confidence.

Key Takeaways:

- Identifying Anxious Attachment Behaviors: This chapter explores anxious attachment patterns such as seeking reassurance and experiencing anxiety in relationships.
- Understanding Triggers: Recognize the triggers that activate anxious responses, such as feelings of inadequacy or perceived distance.
- Tracing Childhood Roots: Reflect on how childhood experiences, like inconsistent caregiving, may have shaped anxious attachment behaviors.
- Building Awareness: Journaling, visualization, and role-play exercises are valuable tools for gaining insight into attachment patterns and fostering self-awareness.

Chapter 4:
The Influence of Childhood on Anxious Attachment

Our early relationships with caregivers play a critical role in shaping our emotional, social, and psychological development. From infancy through childhood, we depend on caregivers for love, support, and guidance, and the quality of these relationships can have long-lasting effects on our sense of self, ability to form healthy relationships, and overall well-being. This section explores the significance of early caregiver relationships and their impact on development.

Attachment Theory and Its Importance

Developed by psychologist John Bowlby, attachment theory offers a framework to understand how early relationships influence development. Infants form attachment bonds with their primary caregivers, usually parents or close family members. These bonds are evident in behaviors such as seeking closeness to the caregiver, looking for comfort during distress, and using the caregiver as a secure base for exploration.

Types of Attachment

Based on research by Bowlby and Mary Ainsworth, attachment theory identifies four primary attachment styles that develop in response to the quality of interactions with caregivers:

1. **Secure Attachment**: Children with secure attachment feel confident their caregivers will meet their needs. They freely explore their environment, knowing they can rely on their caregiver for support. As a result, they develop positive self-esteem, trusting relationships, and effective coping mechanisms.
2. **Anxious-Ambivalent Attachment**: Children with this attachment style may be clingy or overly demanding toward caregivers, showing anxiety about separation and difficulty self-soothing. This can lead to challenges with self-esteem, trust, and emotional regulation in future relationships.

3. **Anxious-Avoidant Attachment**: Children with anxious-avoidant attachment often appear detached or indifferent to caregivers. They may avoid seeking comfort and prefer to explore independently, which may result in fear of intimacy and difficulties expressing emotions in relationships.
4. **Disorganized Attachment**: This attachment style is marked by erratic or confused behaviors toward caregivers. Children may show fear or apprehension and struggle to form coherent attachment strategies, leading to difficulties in building stable relationships in adulthood.

Impact on Development

The quality of early relationships significantly influences various aspects of development, including:

1. **Emotional Regulation**: Secure attachments foster healthy emotional regulation, allowing individuals to manage stress and negative emotions effectively. Insecure attachments can lead to difficulties in managing emotions and stress.
2. **Social Skills**: Securely attached individuals often develop strong social skills, including empathy, communication, and conflict resolution. Insecure attachment can hinder these skills, leading to challenges in forming and maintaining relationships.
3. **Self-Esteem**: Secure attachment promotes a strong sense of self-worth, resulting in higher self-esteem and confidence. Insecure attachment can contribute to low self-esteem and feelings of inadequacy.
4. **Interpersonal Relationships**: Early relationships with caregivers serve as a blueprint for future relationships. Those with secure attachments tend to form stable and fulfilling relationships in adulthood, while insecure attachments can lead to challenges in building and maintaining healthy connections.

Attachment Trauma and Its Emotional Impact

Attachment trauma refers to disruptions in early attachment relationships that negatively affect emotional and psychological well-being. This can result from neglect, abuse, or inconsistent caregiving. Attachment trauma can have lasting consequences, including difficulties in trusting others, emotional dysregulation, low self-esteem, and trouble forming close relationships.

Understanding Attachment Trauma

Attachment trauma occurs when a child's need for safety and nurturing is disrupted due to various forms of maltreatment, such as:

1. **Neglect**: A lack of consistent caregiving can make children feel abandoned, unworthy, and unlovable.
2. **Abuse**: Physical, emotional, or sexual abuse disrupts attachment bonds and can lead to difficulties with intimacy, trust, and self-esteem.
3. **Separation**: Prolonged or repeated separations from caregivers, such as through hospitalization or divorce, can result in feelings of abandonment and anxiety.
4. **Inconsistent Caregiving**: Unpredictable caregiving can create confusion and distress, undermining the child's sense of stability and safety.

Impact on Emotional Development

Attachment trauma can have profound effects on emotional development, leading to:

1. **Difficulty Trusting Others**: Those who experience attachment trauma may struggle to trust others, fearing rejection or betrayal.
2. **Emotional Dysregulation**: Trauma can disrupt the development of emotional regulation skills, leading to unpredictable emotional responses.
3. **Low Self-Esteem**: Trauma can erode self-worth, leading to feelings of inadequacy and self-blame.
4. **Difficulty Forming Close Relationships**: People with attachment trauma may avoid vulnerability or push others away to protect themselves from further emotional pain.

Strategies for Healing from Attachment Trauma

Healing from attachment trauma involves self-awareness, self-compassion, and therapeutic support. Effective strategies include:

1. **Therapy**: Trauma-informed therapy can help individuals explore and process past traumas while developing healthier coping mechanisms.
2. **Mindfulness and Self-Compassion**: Mindfulness practices encourage self-acceptance and present-moment awareness, helping individuals build resilience.
3. **Building Supportive Relationships**: Engaging in healthy relationships based on trust and mutual respect can foster healing from past attachment wounds.
4. **Exploring Attachment Patterns**: Understanding one's attachment patterns can empower individuals to challenge maladaptive behaviors and foster growth.

Long-Term Effects of Attachment Trauma on Adult Relationships

Attachment trauma experienced in childhood can have lasting effects on adult relationships. These effects manifest in insecure attachment styles, such as:

1. **Anxious Attachment**: Individuals may exhibit clingy behavior, seek constant reassurance, and struggle with emotional dependency.
2. **Avoidant Attachment**: People may prioritize independence, avoid emotional intimacy, and struggle to express emotions in relationships.
3. **Disorganized Attachment**: Erratic behavior in relationships can occur, as individuals oscillate between seeking closeness and withdrawing emotionally.

Patterns of Behavior in Adult Relationships

Attachment trauma can lead to behaviors such as:

1. **Fear of Abandonment**: Fear of being left alone may cause individuals to cling to or push away partners.
2. **Difficulty Trusting Others**: Individuals may view relationships through a lens of suspicion and mistrust, making it hard to believe in their partner's intentions.
3. **Emotional Dysregulation**: Difficulty managing emotions can result in intense conflicts and misunderstandings in relationships.

4. **Self-Sabotage**: Some individuals may engage in behaviors that undermine their relationships, such as withdrawing emotionally or creating conflict, due to fears of vulnerability.

By recognizing the impact of attachment trauma, individuals can work toward healing and building healthier relationships, fostering resilience, self-awareness, and emotional stability.

Strategies for Healing and Growth

Although the long-term effects of attachment trauma on adult relationships can be profound, healing and personal growth are possible through effort, time, and support. Below are some strategies for fostering healing and cultivating healthier relationships:

1. **Therapy**
    Working with a trauma-informed therapist can provide a safe environment to explore past traumas, process emotions, and develop healthier coping mechanisms. Therapy can help individuals understand how attachment trauma has shaped their relationships and guide them in making positive changes.
2. **Self-Reflection**
    Engaging in self-reflection allows individuals to recognize and challenge maladaptive behaviors rooted in their attachment styles. By understanding the origin of their attachment patterns, individuals can make more intentional choices in how they approach relationships.
3. **Communication Skills**
    Developing effective communication skills, such as active listening, assertiveness, and empathy, can help navigate conflicts and misunderstandings. By expressing needs and feelings openly, individuals can build stronger, more authentic connections with their partners.
4. **Building Supportive Relationships**
    Forming a supportive network of friends, family, or support groups can provide essential validation and empathy. Supportive relationships help individuals feel less isolated and encourage them as they work toward healing and growth.

Key Takeaways:

- **Impact of Early Caregiving**: This chapter highlights how early caregiving experiences, such as responsiveness and emotional availability, shape attachment patterns, including anxious attachment.
- **Inconsistent Caregiving**: Inconsistent or unpredictable caregiving can contribute to anxious attachment, leading to heightened anxiety and insecurity in later relationships.
- **Attachment Figures**: The role of primary caregivers, usually parents, in shaping a child's sense of security, trust, and self-worth, which influences future relationship dynamics.
- **Parenting Styles**: How different parenting styles (authoritarian, permissive, neglectful) impact attachment development, particularly in forming anxious attachment patterns.
- **Interpersonal Relationships**: Early social interactions with peers and significant others also shape attachment patterns and influence later relational dynamics.
- **Internal Working Models**: Early attachment experiences create internalized beliefs about oneself, others, and relationships, influencing thoughts and behaviors in adulthood.
- **Trauma and Adversity**: The effect of childhood trauma and adversity on attachment development, particularly the increased vulnerability to anxious attachment patterns.

Action Steps/Call to Action:

- Reflect on how your childhood experiences may have influenced your attachment style.
- Consider how your early caregiving and relationship patterns have shaped your beliefs and behaviors in adult relationships.

Stay tuned for the next chapter, where we'll explore strategies for healing from childhood experiences and cultivating greater security and fulfillment in adult relationships

Chapter 5:
The Neuroscience of Anxious Attachment

Understanding Neuroplasticity and Its Role in Positive Change

Neuroplasticity refers to the brain's extraordinary ability to reorganize itself by creating new neural pathways throughout life. This capacity for change provides immense potential for personal growth, healing, and transformation. In this section, we will explore the concept of neuroplasticity and how embracing this capability can promote positive change in various areas of life.

What is Neuroplasticity?

Neuroplasticity challenges the outdated belief that the brain is a rigid, unchangeable organ. Instead, it demonstrates that the brain is highly adaptable, constantly changing its structure and function in response to learning, experiences, and environmental influences. Neuroplasticity is an ongoing process where new synapses form, old connections are pruned, and neural pathways are reorganized to adapt to new demands.

Harnessing Neuroplasticity for Positive Change

Neuroplasticity offers a framework for personal development and self-improvement by enabling individuals to change their thinking, behaviors, and emotional responses. Below are key ways to utilize neuroplasticity to foster growth:

1. **Mindfulness and Meditation**
   Mindfulness practices, such as meditation and mindful breathing, strengthen connections in brain areas related to attention, emotional regulation, and self-awareness. Consistent mindfulness practice enhances cognitive flexibility and resilience, allowing individuals to handle stress and adversity more effectively.

2. **Learning and Skill Development**
   Engaging in activities that involve learning new skills or acquiring knowledge promotes the formation of new neural connections. Whether learning a new language, playing an instrument, or picking up a new hobby, challenging the brain with novel tasks enhances cognitive growth and adaptability.
3. **Therapeutic Interventions**
   Therapy, such as cognitive-behavioral therapy (CBT) or mindfulness-based approaches, harnesses neuroplasticity to rewire maladaptive thought patterns and behaviors. Therapeutic interventions help individuals heal emotional wounds, develop healthier coping strategies, and promote long-lasting change.
4. **Physical Exercise**
   Regular physical activity boosts neuroplasticity by increasing brain-derived neurotrophic factor (BDNF), a protein that supports the growth and survival of neurons. Aerobic exercise, in particular, encourages neurogenesis (the creation of new neurons) and improves cognitive functioning and mood.
5. **Positive Social Interactions**
   Building meaningful social connections supports neuroplasticity and overall well-being. Positive social interactions trigger the release of oxytocin, a hormone that fosters bonding and reduces stress, facilitating neural growth and improving emotional resilience.

The Role of Belief and Intention in Neuroplasticity

A growth mindset is critical in leveraging neuroplasticity for positive change. By believing in the brain's potential to adapt, individuals create the conditions necessary for growth. Setting clear intentions and goals for self-improvement activates the brain's motivation circuits, priming it for the changes that lie ahead.

Embracing neuroplasticity as a powerful tool for healing and personal growth means understanding that change is always possible. Whether through mindfulness, learning new skills, therapy, exercise, or nurturing relationships, neuroplasticity empowers individuals to reshape their minds and lives in meaningful ways.

Brain Regions Involved in Neuroplasticity

Several brain regions are responsible for facilitating neuroplasticity and adapting to new experiences. Understanding these key areas helps illuminate how the brain evolves and supports change over time:

1. **Hippocampus**
   This seahorse-shaped structure plays a crucial role in memory formation and learning. Neuroplasticity in the hippocampus is essential for encoding new information and adapting to new environments.

2. **Prefrontal Cortex**
   Located in the brain's frontal lobe, the prefrontal cortex is involved in decision-making, impulse control, and regulating social behavior. Neuroplasticity in this region allows for better emotional regulation and adaptability.

3. **Amygdala**
   The amygdala, responsible for processing emotions such as fear and anxiety, plays a role in emotional memory and stress responses. Neuroplasticity in the amygdala influences how individuals process and manage emotions.

4. **Basal Ganglia**
   Involved in motor control, habit formation, and reward processing, the basal ganglia play a role in learning motor skills and reinforcing behavioral patterns.

5. **Neocortex**
   The neocortex is essential for higher cognitive functions like language, perception, and abstract thinking. Neuroplasticity in this region supports learning and memory across various domains.

6. **Dopaminergic Pathways**
   These pathways regulate reward-based learning and motivation. Neuroplasticity here influences the brain's response to reward and reinforcement, impacting behaviors like addiction and goal-seeking.

Neurochemical Processes in Neuroplasticity

Neuroplasticity is driven by intricate neurochemical processes, including the release and regulation of neurotransmitters and neuromodulators. Some of these processes include:

1. **Neurotransmitter Release**
   Neurotransmitters such as glutamate, dopamine, and serotonin play key roles in synaptic plasticity, influencing how neurons communicate and adapt over time.
2. **Synaptic Plasticity**
   Processes like long-term potentiation (LTP) and long-term depression (LTD) strengthen or weaken synaptic connections, contributing to learning and memory formation.
3. **Neurotrophic Factors**
   Proteins like brain-derived neurotrophic factor (BDNF) promote the survival and growth of neurons, facilitating neural adaptation and cognitive function.
4. **Modulation of Neurotransmitter Systems**
   Neuromodulators like dopamine and serotonin regulate mood, motivation, and emotional responses, influencing synaptic plasticity in the process.
5. **Epigenetic Regulation**
   Epigenetic mechanisms, which modify gene expression without altering DNA, affect neuroplasticity by shaping the brain's response to environmental stimuli and experience.

Neuroplasticity and Healing

The brain's ability to adapt and reorganize through neuroplasticity plays a vital role in recovery from trauma, injury, or illness. Some key aspects include:

1. **Compensation for Damage**
   Neuroplasticity allows the brain to compensate for damage by rewiring neural pathways, enabling individuals to regain lost abilities after injury or stroke.
2. **Rehabilitation and Training**
   Rehabilitation programs leverage neuroplasticity through targeted therapies that promote relearning of skills, motor functions, and cognitive abilities.
3. **Emotional Resilience**
   Practices such as mindfulness and cognitive-behavioral therapy help reshape the brain's emotional regulation systems, promoting resilience and psychological well-being.

Key Takeaways

- **The Brain's Adaptability**: Neuroplasticity allows the brain to adapt in response to experiences, learning, and environmental changes.
- **Practical Applications**: Techniques like mindfulness, learning new skills, and engaging in therapy can foster neuroplasticity and promote personal growth.
- **Healing and Recovery**: Neuroplasticity supports recovery from injury, trauma, and emotional challenges, offering hope for rehabilitation and well-being.

Action Steps/Call to Action:

- Embrace opportunities for lifelong learning, self-reflection, and skill development to harness neuroplasticity.
- Incorporate regular mindfulness practices, physical activity, and positive social interactions to promote brain growth.
- Believe in your capacity to change and grow, setting clear goals and intentions for personal development.

In the next section, we'll explore how neuroplasticity can be applied to enhance emotional regulation and relationship dynamics, particularly in the context of anxious attachment.

Mindfulness and the Brain: Strengthening Attachment Pathways Through Simple Practices

Mindfulness—the practice of being present and aware of one's thoughts, emotions, and sensations without judgment—can have a transformative impact on the brain's attachment pathways. By regularly engaging in mindfulness, we can strengthen the neural circuits related to secure attachment, promoting emotional regulation, empathy, and connection. This section outlines several mindfulness practices and their effects on the brain's attachment pathways.

1. Mindful Breathing

To practice mindful breathing, sit comfortably and focus on the sensations of your breath. Notice each inhale and exhale, paying attention to the rise and fall of your chest or the feeling of air moving through your nostrils. If your mind wanders, acknowledge the distraction and gently bring your attention back to your breath. This simple practice strengthens neural pathways responsible for attention and emotional regulation, fostering calmness and presence.

2. Loving-Kindness Meditation

Loving-kindness meditation focuses on cultivating compassion for oneself and others. Begin by imagining a loved one and silently repeat affirmations such as "May you be happy, may you be healthy, may you be safe." Feel any sensations of warmth and openness as you extend these wishes. This meditation activates brain regions related to empathy and social connection, enhancing feelings of warmth, compassion, and affection towards yourself and others.

3. Body Scan Meditation

In this practice, you systematically bring awareness to each part of your body, starting from your head and moving down to your toes. Focus on any sensations, tension, or discomfort, gradually moving your attention from one area to the next. This practice improves interoceptive awareness—the ability to sense internal bodily experiences—by strengthening neural pathways linked to self-awareness and emotional regulation.

4. Gratitude Practice

Gratitude practice involves reflecting on things you appreciate, such as supportive relationships, small acts of kindness, or beautiful moments in nature. As you focus on each item, notice any feelings of joy or warmth that arise. Gratitude activates brain regions involved in reward processing and positive emotions, promoting a sense of well-being and connection.

5. Mindful Movement

Mindful movement, such as yoga or tai chi, involves bringing awareness to the body as it moves through different postures or sequences. Focus on your breath and bodily sensations, observing any tension or resistance. This practice enhances body awareness and emotional regulation, grounding you in the present moment while promoting emotional stability.

Key Takeaways:

- **Brain Regions Involved**: This chapter explores the neuroscience behind anxious attachment, focusing on brain structures such as the amygdala, prefrontal cortex, and HPA axis, which regulate emotional responses and attachment behaviors.
- **Fear and Threat Response**: Individuals with anxious attachment tend to have heightened activation in the brain's fear centers, like the amygdala. This sensitivity can lead to exaggerated emotional reactions to perceived threats of abandonment or rejection.
- **Cortisol and Stress Response**: Chronic stress, and the resulting elevated cortisol levels, can dysregulate the HPA axis, further intensifying anxious attachment behaviors.
- **Attachment and Reward Systems**: The brain's reward system, involving dopamine and oxytocin, plays a role in attachment. People with anxious attachment may seek validation to trigger the reward system, temporarily alleviating insecurity.
- **Impact of Early Experiences**: Early caregiving experiences help shape the neural circuits involved in attachment. The critical period during childhood determines the foundation for future attachment behaviors.
- **Plasticity and Change**: Despite the neural wiring of anxious attachment, the brain's plasticity allows for change. Therapy, mindfulness, and positive relational experiences can promote more secure attachment patterns.
- **Gene-Environment Interactions**: Genetic predispositions interact with environmental factors, shaping attachment behaviors and neural development. This interplay can influence how attachment patterns form and manifest in adulthood.

Action Steps/Call to Action:

- Reflect on how the neuroscience of anxious attachment resonates with your experiences in relationships.
- Engage in mindfulness practices or therapy to foster emotional regulation and neuroplasticity.

Stay tuned for the next chapter, where we will delve into "Coping Mechanisms and Maladaptive Behaviors," exploring practical strategies for managing emotions, stress, and cultivating security in relationships.

Chapter 6:
Managing Emotions and Unhealthy Behavioral Patterns

Maladaptive behaviors are ineffective or harmful actions used to cope with challenges or emotional distress. These patterns, often rooted in learned responses, fail to achieve desired outcomes and can hinder well-being. This section explores common maladaptive behaviors, their underlying mechanisms, and strategies for overcoming these unhealthy patterns.

1. **Avoidance** Avoidance is a coping mechanism where individuals evade situations, thoughts, or emotions that cause anxiety or discomfort. While it may offer temporary relief, avoidance exacerbates the issues it seeks to avoid, often leading to worsened mental health over time.
   - **Manifestations of Avoidance:**
     - **Social Avoidance**: Individuals may avoid social interactions due to fear of rejection, leading to loneliness and relationship difficulties.
     - **Avoidance of Responsibilities**: Procrastination or neglecting tasks due to fear of failure or overwhelm can lead to missed opportunities and increased stress.
     - **Emotional Avoidance**: People may suppress emotions or distract themselves to avoid confronting their feelings, which impairs emotional regulation.
     - **Avoidance of Triggers**: Avoiding places or situations that remind individuals of past trauma reinforces fear and anxiety over time.
   - **Underlying Mechanisms:**
     - **Fear and Anxiety**: Avoidance is often driven by fear and discomfort, with individuals withdrawing to avoid distress.
     - **Negative Reinforcement**: Avoiding distressing stimuli provides temporary relief, reinforcing the avoidance behavior.

- **Cognitive Distortions**: Individuals may overestimate threats or their inability to cope, leading to further avoidance.
  - **Impacts**:
    - **Interpersonal Difficulties**: Avoidance damages relationships, creating feelings of isolation.
    - **Maintenance of Anxiety**: The more one avoids, the more anxiety is reinforced.
    - **Decreased Life Quality**: Avoidance limits opportunities for growth and personal fulfillment.
  - **Strategies to Overcome Avoidance**:
    - **Identify Triggers**: Recognize situations that provoke avoidance to better manage them.
    - **Challenge Negative Beliefs**: Replace catastrophic thoughts with more balanced perspectives.
    - **Gradual Exposure**: Face feared situations in small steps to build tolerance and confidence.
    - **Relaxation Techniques**: Use methods like deep breathing and mindfulness to reduce anxiety.
    - **Seek Support**: Reach out to a therapist or loved ones for encouragement.

2. **Perfectionism** Perfectionism involves setting excessively high standards and striving for flawlessness. It becomes harmful when it leads to chronic self-criticism, stress, and fear of failure.
   - **Manifestations**:
     - **Excessive Self-Criticism**: Perfectionists harshly judge themselves for any perceived shortcomings.
     - **Fear of Failure**: The fear of making mistakes often paralyzes individuals from pursuing new challenges.
     - **Procrastination**: Anxiety about not achieving perfection can lead to putting off tasks.
     - **Rigidity**: Perfectionists often resist flexibility, insisting on doing things their way.
   - **Underlying Mechanisms**:

- **Conditional Self-Worth**: Perfectionists may believe their worth depends on achieving high standards.
- **Cognitive Distortions**: All-or-nothing thinking exacerbates the unrealistic expectations.
- **External Validation**: Seeking approval from others to validate one's self-worth perpetuates the cycle of perfectionism.
  - **Strategies to Overcome Perfectionism**:
    - **Set Realistic Goals**: Focus on progress rather than perfection.
    - **Practice Self-Compassion**: Treat yourself with kindness and patience when making mistakes.
    - **Challenge Perfectionistic Thinking**: Replace rigid thinking with more flexible perspectives.
    - **Seek Support**: Counseling or therapy can provide tools to manage perfectionism.

3. **People-Pleasing** People-pleasing is the tendency to prioritize others' needs over one's own, often at the expense of personal boundaries.
   - **Manifestations**:
     - **Over-commitment**: Taking on too many obligations to avoid saying no.
     - **Seeking Approval**: Constantly needing validation from others.
     - **Avoiding Conflict**: Fear of confrontation leads people-pleasers to suppress their feelings.
   - **Underlying Motivations**:
     - **Fear of Rejection**: People-pleasers often fear disapproval or being disliked.
     - **Low Self-Esteem**: Seeking validation from others to feel valued.
     - **Need for Control**: Pleasing others helps maintain perceived control over relationships.
   - **Strategies to Overcome People-Pleasing**:
     - **Practice Assertiveness**: Learn to say no respectfully and set boundaries.
     - **Self-Reflection**: Understand the motivations behind people-pleasing behavior.

- **Build Self-Esteem**: Cultivate self-worth that isn't dependent on external validation.
4. **Self-Sabotage** Self-sabotage involves engaging in behaviors that undermine one's own success or well-being.
    - **Manifestations**:
        - **Procrastination**: Avoiding tasks that are essential for achieving goals.
        - **Self-Doubt**: Negative self-talk that undermines confidence.
        - **Avoidance of Success**: Fearing the responsibilities that come with success.
    - **Underlying Mechanisms**:
        - **Fear of Failure**: Self-sabotaging behavior serves as a protective mechanism against disappointment.
        - **Fear of Success**: Success may bring unknown challenges, which can be frightening.
        - **Low Self-Esteem**: Individuals may not feel deserving of success.
    - **Strategies to Overcome Self-Sabotage**:
        - **Increase Self-Awareness**: Identify patterns of self-sabotage.
        - **Challenge Negative Beliefs**: Replace limiting beliefs with affirmations of self-worth.
        - **Set Realistic Goals**: Break tasks into achievable steps.
5. **Escapism** Escapism involves avoiding reality through excessive engagement in distractions like substance abuse, gaming, or binge-watching TV.
    - **Manifestations**:
        - **Excessive Screen Time**: Spending disproportionate time on digital distractions.
        - **Fantasy and Daydreaming**: Retreating into imagined worlds to avoid dealing with real-life problems.
    - **Underlying Motivations**:
        - **Stress and Anxiety**: Escapism provides temporary relief from emotional distress.
        - **Boredom**: Seeking excitement through distractions.
    - **Strategies to Overcome Escapism**:
        - **Mindful Awareness**: Recognize when escapism is interfering with responsibilities.

- **Address Underlying Issues**: Face the problems that are driving the desire to escape.

By addressing maladaptive behaviors and adopting healthier coping mechanisms, individuals can promote emotional stability, self-awareness, and well-being.

Overcoming Maladaptive Behaviors

Breaking free from maladaptive behaviors is a journey that requires self-awareness, compassion, and commitment to change. Here are strategies that can help individuals overcome harmful patterns and cultivate healthier behaviors:

1. **Self-Reflection**: Start by reflecting on the maladaptive behaviors present in your life. Identify the triggers, emotions, and thoughts that lead to these behaviors. Consider the underlying fears or beliefs that fuel them.
2. **Challenge Negative Thoughts**: Use cognitive restructuring to challenge negative thoughts that contribute to maladaptive behaviors. Replace unhelpful or distorted beliefs with balanced, realistic perspectives.
3. **Develop Coping Skills**: Build healthier coping mechanisms, such as mindfulness, relaxation techniques, and assertiveness. These tools help manage stress and difficult emotions without resorting to maladaptive behaviors.
4. **Set Realistic Goals**: Focus on progress, not perfection. Set achievable goals, and be kind to yourself when setbacks occur. Celebrate small victories along the way.
5. **Seek Support**: Reach out to supportive friends, family, or mental health professionals. Therapy can provide guidance in addressing underlying issues and developing stronger coping strategies.

By understanding and addressing maladaptive behaviors, people can break free from destructive patterns, cultivating greater self-esteem, resilience, and well-being. With patience, dedication, and the right support, positive change and a more fulfilling life are within reach.

Key Takeaways:

- **Coping Strategies**: This chapter explores how individuals with anxious attachment may cope with relationship anxiety through mechanisms like seeking reassurance, people-pleasing, or avoiding conflict. These behaviors often reflect underlying insecurity and the need for external validation.
- **Short-Term Relief vs. Long-Term Solutions**: While maladaptive coping mechanisms may offer temporary relief, they can ultimately perpetuate harmful patterns. The chapter helps readers distinguish between adaptive coping that fosters growth and maladaptive behaviors that lead to long-term relationship challenges.
- **Escalation of Anxiety**: The chapter discusses how certain behaviors—such as avoidance, clinginess, or control—can escalate anxiety in relationships, creating a cycle of dependency, conflict, and emotional distress.
- **Understanding Triggers**: By recognizing specific triggers that activate maladaptive behaviors—such as perceived rejection or abandonment—readers can develop healthier responses that promote emotional regulation and relationship satisfaction.
- **Breaking Free from Patterns**: Through self-awareness and reflection, readers are encouraged to challenge the fears and beliefs that drive maladaptive behaviors. With intention, individuals can break free from destructive patterns and adopt healthier relational strategies.
- **Seeking Support**: The chapter highlights the importance of seeking help from trusted individuals or professionals to explore healthier ways of managing anxiety and insecurity.
- **Self-Compassion and Forgiveness**: Practicing self-compassion and forgiving oneself for past mistakes is essential to overcoming maladaptive behaviors. Embracing these qualities promotes self-acceptance, emotional resilience, and personal growth.

Action Steps/Call to Action:

- **Reflect on Your Coping Mechanisms**: Take time to assess how you handle anxiety and insecurity in your relationships. Are your coping mechanisms effective, or do they cause more harm than good?
- **Identify Maladaptive Patterns**: Pinpoint specific behaviors or patterns that may be limiting your personal

growth or harming your relationships. Consider how these behaviors may be reinforcing feelings of insecurity or stress.

Stay tuned for the next chapter, where we will dive into practical strategies for transforming maladaptive coping mechanisms into healthier, adaptive responses that promote emotional security and fulfillment in relationships.

Chapter 7:

The Effect of Anxious Attachment on Intimate Relationships

Relationship dynamics with a romantic partner revolve around the emotions, behaviors, and communication patterns that define the connection between two people. To build and maintain a healthy, fulfilling relationship, a strong foundation of trust, open communication, mutual respect, and emotional intimacy is essential. In this section, we will explore the critical factors contributing to relationship strength and longevity, along with strategies for managing common challenges and fostering deeper connection.

Key Components of Relationship Dynamics

1. **Trust**:
   Trust is the cornerstone of any successful romantic relationship. It involves believing in your partner's reliability, honesty, and commitment to the relationship. Building trust requires transparency, consistent communication, and following through on promises. Demonstrating trustworthiness fosters a secure and stable bond.
2. **Communication**:
   Effective communication is crucial for expressing needs, resolving conflicts, and fostering emotional closeness. Active listening, empathy, and assertiveness allow couples to navigate challenges while maintaining their connection. Open and honest dialogue strengthens understanding and helps manage differences constructively.
3. **Emotional Intimacy**:
   Emotional intimacy entails sharing your vulnerabilities, fears, and dreams with your partner and feeling validated and accepted. This deepens the emotional bond and enhances the sense of closeness. Cultivating emotional intimacy involves being emotionally available, empathetic, and attuned to each other's needs.
4. **Respect and Mutual Support**:
   A healthy relationship is built on mutual respect and support. Partners should honor each other's individuality,

boundaries, and autonomy. Offering encouragement, celebrating successes, and being present during challenges fosters a sense of partnership and belonging.

Managing Common Challenges in Relationships

1. **Conflict Resolution**:
   Conflicts are a natural part of any relationship, but the way they are handled can either strengthen or weaken the bond. Successful conflict resolution focuses on finding solutions rather than blaming. Partners should practice active listening, show empathy, and be willing to compromise to resolve disagreements constructively.
2. **Maintaining Independence**:
   While romantic relationships involve a deep emotional connection, it's vital for both individuals to maintain their independence and personal identity. Healthy relationship dynamics support personal growth and self-expression, allowing partners to pursue individual interests without feeling confined or controlled.
3. **Managing Differences**:
   Partners may have different personalities, preferences, and communication styles, which can sometimes lead to misunderstandings. Learning to accept, appreciate, and celebrate these differences is key to fostering a respectful and harmonious relationship. Finding a balance between compromise and maintaining individual uniqueness strengthens the relationship.
4. **Navigating Life Transitions**:
   Life transitions, such as moving in together, starting a family, or changing careers, can bring stress or uncertainty into a relationship. During these times, open communication and mutual support are crucial. Couples should adapt to changes together, reinforcing their commitment and working collaboratively to navigate these transitions.

Action Steps/Call to Action:

- Reflect on how trust, communication, emotional intimacy, and mutual respect are being cultivated in your relationship.
- Identify any common challenges or conflicts in your relationship and consider strategies for addressing them

through constructive communication and mutual understanding.

Stay engaged for the next chapter, where we will explore **"Practical Tools for Strengthening Relationship Bonds"** and strategies for nurturing connection and resilience in your partnership.

Strategies for Promoting Healthy Relationship Dynamics

1. **Prioritize Communication**:
   Make communication the cornerstone of your relationship by regularly checking in, expressing appreciation, and addressing concerns as they arise. Practice active listening, empathy, and open dialogue to fully understand your partner's perspective. Address conflicts constructively to strengthen emotional connection.
2. **Cultivate Trust**:
   Build and maintain trust by being honest, transparent, and reliable. Avoid behaviors that could damage trust, such as dishonesty or secrecy. Trust develops over time through consistent, trustworthy actions and open communication, reinforcing the security of the relationship.
3. **Create Rituals of Connection**:
   Establish regular rituals of connection, such as weekly date nights, shared hobbies, or meaningful conversations, to nurture emotional intimacy. These rituals provide opportunities for quality time, reminding both partners of the importance of the relationship and reinforcing their bond.
4. **Practice Empathy and Understanding**:
   Strengthen your relationship by practicing empathy—put yourself in your partner's shoes and validate their emotions. Show compassion and offer support in difficult times, while also celebrating successes together. Empathy fosters deeper emotional intimacy and mutual respect.
5. **Seek Professional Support**:
   If challenges arise that feel difficult to navigate alone, consider seeking help from a couples therapist or relationship counselor. Professional guidance can offer tools for improving communication, resolving conflicts, and deepening your connection.

By focusing on trust, communication, empathy, and mutual respect, couples can create a strong, healthy partnership that endures. Building a fulfilling relationship requires ongoing effort, but with commitment and teamwork, it is possible to create a loving, supportive bond that enhances both partners' lives.

Exploring Communication Patterns: Improving Connection and Understanding in Relationships

Communication patterns are vital in shaping the dynamics of romantic relationships, influencing emotional intimacy, conflict resolution, and overall connection. Effective communication fosters mutual understanding and strengthens the bond between partners, while poor communication can lead to misunderstandings and distance. In this section, we will explore common communication styles, their impact on relationships, and strategies for promoting healthy communication.

Common Communication Patterns:

1. **Assertive Communication**:
   Assertive communication is characterized by expressing thoughts, feelings, and needs clearly and respectfully. Assertive communicators are confident in expressing themselves while considering the feelings and rights of their partner. This style fosters mutual respect, active listening, and collaborative problem-solving, which strengthens relationship dynamics and emotional intimacy.
2. **Passive Communication**:
   Passive communication involves suppressing one's thoughts, feelings, or needs to avoid conflict or discomfort. People who communicate passively often have difficulty asserting themselves, which can lead to unmet needs, frustration, and built-up resentment. In relationships, passive communication may prioritize short-term harmony but can result in long-term dissatisfaction and emotional disconnection.
3. **Aggressive Communication**:
   Aggressive communication is marked by dominance, hostility, or the use of intimidation to assert control. This communication style often involves harsh language, insults, or blame. Aggressive communication damages trust, creates

fear, and harms emotional safety, leaving both partners feeling misunderstood or attacked, which weakens the relationship.

4. **Passive-Aggressive Communication**:
   Passive-aggressive communication expresses negative emotions indirectly through sarcasm, avoidance, or subtle actions rather than openly addressing issues. This communication style often leads to frustration, confusion, and unresolved conflict, eroding trust and fostering resentment in relationships.

Impact of Communication Patterns on Relationships:

- **Assertive Communication**: Builds trust, fosters healthy conflict resolution, and strengthens emotional intimacy. It encourages open dialogue and promotes a positive, supportive relationship dynamic.
- **Passive Communication**: Leads to unresolved issues, feelings of neglect, and a lack of personal fulfillment. Over time, this can weaken the bond between partners and create emotional distance.
- **Aggressive Communication**: Creates an atmosphere of fear and mistrust, pushing partners apart and damaging emotional safety. It can result in frequent conflicts and hinder the development of a healthy, supportive relationship.
- **Passive-Aggressive Communication**: Causes confusion and perpetuates hidden resentment. This communication style can prevent meaningful conflict resolution and hinder emotional intimacy.

Strategies for Promoting Healthy Communication:

1. **Cultivate Assertiveness**: Practice expressing your needs, feelings, and boundaries directly and respectfully. Assertive communication fosters mutual respect and understanding, ensuring that both partners feel heard and valued in the relationship.
2. **Active Listening**: Focus on truly hearing your partner's words without interrupting or formulating a response while they speak. Active listening shows empathy and creates a sense of emotional safety, which strengthens the relationship.

3. **Address Issues Early**: Avoid letting issues fester by addressing concerns as they arise. Open and timely communication helps prevent resentment and promotes problem-solving in a constructive manner.
4. **Practice Empathy**: Seek to understand your partner's perspective by putting yourself in their shoes. Empathy promotes compassion, deepens emotional intimacy, and helps prevent misunderstandings.
5. **Use "I" Statements**: When discussing concerns, use "I" statements (e.g., "I feel..." or "I need...") to express your emotions and needs without placing blame. This approach helps keep communication constructive and reduces defensiveness.
6. **Stay Calm During Conflict**: In moments of disagreement, strive to remain calm and composed. Escalating arguments or resorting to aggressive communication only damages the relationship, while calm, thoughtful communication leads to better outcomes.

By improving communication patterns and adopting healthy strategies, couples can enhance their connection, promote emotional intimacy, and build a foundation of trust and understanding that will sustain their relationship through challenges.

Impact of Communication Patterns on Relationship Dynamics:

1. **Emotional Intimacy**: Effective communication, especially assertive communication, fosters emotional intimacy by encouraging openness, vulnerability, and mutual understanding between partners. When couples share their thoughts and feelings authentically, it deepens their emotional bond and strengthens the relationship.
2. **Conflict Resolution**: Communication styles directly affect how conflicts are handled. Assertive communication aids in constructive conflict resolution by emphasizing active listening, empathy, and collaboration. In contrast, passive, aggressive, or passive-aggressive communication can escalate tensions, breed resentment, and obstruct resolution efforts.
3. **Trust and Respect**: Open, honest, and respectful communication reinforces trust and respect in a relationship. When partners communicate transparently and value each

other's opinions and feelings, they demonstrate trustworthiness. Conversely, dishonesty, manipulation, or disrespect erodes trust and damages the relationship's foundation.

4. **Emotional Safety**: Healthy communication patterns create an emotionally safe environment, allowing partners to express themselves without fear of judgment or retaliation. Communication styles involving criticism, defensiveness, or stonewalling can inhibit authentic expression and create emotional distance between partners.

Strategies for Promoting Healthy Communication Habits:

1. **Practice Active Listening**: Develop active listening skills by giving your partner your full attention, making eye contact, and validating their feelings. Avoid interrupting or jumping to solutions—focus on understanding their perspective first.

2. **Use "I" Statements**: Express your feelings and needs using "I" statements to avoid sounding accusatory. For example, say, "I feel hurt when I don't receive your attention," rather than, "You always ignore me." This approach fosters a more constructive conversation.

3. **Display Empathy and Understanding**: Show empathy by acknowledging and validating your partner's feelings, even when you disagree. Demonstrating concern and support reinforces emotional connection and trust.

4. **Practice Conflict Resolution Skills**: Approach conflicts with the goal of collaboration, aiming to find solutions that benefit both partners. Avoid personal attacks, criticism, or blame. If emotions become overwhelming, take a break and return to the discussion when both partners are calm.

5. **Seek Feedback and Check-Ins**: Regularly ask your partner for feedback on your communication patterns and how they affect the relationship. Schedule regular check-ins to address challenges, celebrate improvements, and refine communication habits.

By promoting healthy communication built on openness, empathy, and respect, couples can enhance understanding, emotional intimacy, and overall relationship satisfaction. Effective communication requires continuous practice and patience, but the long-term benefits can profoundly enrich your relationship.

Balancing Attachment Needs and Relationship Dynamics: Handling Intimacy and Autonomy

The interplay between attachment needs and relationship dynamics is a crucial factor in shaping the quality and stability of romantic relationships. Our attachment needs, rooted in early experiences with caregivers, influence our desire for emotional closeness, security, and reassurance from our partners. However, navigating these needs within a relationship requires a careful balance between intimacy and autonomy, respect for boundaries, and fostering mutual growth. In this section, we will explore how attachment needs affect relationships and offer strategies to maintain a healthy equilibrium between emotional connection and individual independence.

Attachment Needs in Relationships:

1. **Security and Reassurance**: According to attachment theory, individuals seek security and reassurance from their partners, reflecting the emotional stability once provided by caregivers in childhood. This often translates into a need for closeness, affection, and reliability from romantic partners.
2. **Emotional Intimacy**: Emotional intimacy is a core aspect of attachment, involving vulnerability, sharing fears and desires, and feeling understood and accepted. Emotional intimacy deepens the connection between partners, fostering a lasting bond.
3. **Dependency vs. Autonomy**: While seeking closeness and support is natural, excessive dependency can lead to an imbalance, affecting autonomy and self-esteem. Healthy relationships must navigate the delicate balance between emotional reliance and independence.

Relationship Dynamics and Autonomy:

1. **Individual Identity**: Successful relationships support personal growth and allow individuals to maintain a sense of identity and autonomy. Each partner should have the space to pursue personal goals and interests outside the relationship, nurturing their individuality.

2. **Boundaries and Respect**: Clear communication about boundaries is crucial to preserve autonomy in relationships. Respecting each other's limits without coercion or manipulation ensures that partners feel respected and understood.
3. **Interdependence**: A hallmark of healthy relationships is interdependence, where partners provide emotional support and companionship while maintaining independence. Mutual respect, trust, and collaboration create a balanced dynamic where both partners feel valued.

Strategies for Balancing Attachment Needs and Relationship Dynamics:

1. **Open Communication**: Discuss attachment needs, relationship dynamics, and expectations openly with your partner. Address how to meet each other's emotional needs while respecting personal boundaries and independence.
2. **Develop Emotional Regulation Skills**: Work on emotional regulation to manage insecurities or anxieties that arise from attachment needs. Techniques such as mindfulness, self-reflection, and self-soothing can help you navigate attachment-related challenges with greater stability.
3. **Set Healthy Boundaries**: Establish clear boundaries that promote both closeness and autonomy. Communicate these boundaries assertively to maintain a sense of self within the relationship.
4. **Prioritize Self-Care**: Engage in self-care practices and activities outside the relationship that bring personal fulfillment. Pursuing hobbies and personal goals helps maintain a strong sense of identity, which enhances emotional well-being.
5. **Seek Professional Support**: If attachment challenges persist, consider counseling or therapy to explore deeper issues and develop strategies for handling attachment needs and fostering a healthy relationship dynamic.

Key Takeaways:

- **Strained Communication**: This chapter explores how anxious attachment patterns can affect communication dynamics. Individuals with anxious attachment may struggle to express their needs assertively, fearing rejection or abandonment, which can lead to misunderstandings and conflicts.

- **Conflict Resolution**: Heightened anxiety in anxious attachment can complicate conflict resolution, leading individuals to avoid or escalate conflicts. Constructive dialogue is often difficult, requiring greater effort to manage anxiety.
- **Emotional Rollercoaster**: The chapter describes the intense emotional fluctuations typical of relationships affected by anxious attachment, where individuals experience emotional highs and lows, cycling between affection and insecurity.
- **Dependency vs. Independence**: Anxious attachment often creates a struggle between seeking emotional closeness and fearing a loss of autonomy. Understanding this balance is critical for personal and relational growth.
- **Impact on Partner**: Partners of individuals with anxious attachment may feel overwhelmed by constant reassurance needs or uncertain about their ability to meet their partner's emotional needs, which can strain the relationship.
- **Cycle of Dysregulation**: Anxiety and insecurity can perpetuate maladaptive behaviors, creating a feedback loop that further strains the relationship and reinforces negative beliefs.
- **Intimacy and Trust**: Despite these challenges, anxious attachment can lead to profound intimacy and trust if both partners commit to mutual understanding, empathy, and personal growth.

Action Steps/Call to Action:

- Reflect on how your attachment patterns may influence your intimate relationships, particularly in terms of communication, conflict resolution, and emotional experiences.
- Consider how your attachment style impacts your partner and the overall dynamics of the relationship.

Stay tuned for the next chapter, where we will explore practical strategies for managing the complexities of intimate relationships affected by anxious attachment and promoting greater security and fulfillment for both partners.

Chapter 8:

Fostering Secure Attachment: Building Trust, Embracing Vulnerability, and Strengthening Connection

To develop secure attachment in relationships, it's essential to deepen self-awareness, foster emotional growth, and cultivate meaningful connections with partners. A secure attachment is characterized by trust, emotional safety, and the ability to embrace vulnerability without fear of rejection or abandonment. This discussion explores strategies to strengthen secure attachment, reduce stress, and enhance emotional bonds.

Understanding Secure Attachment:

1. **Trust and Dependability:** Secure attachment is built on trust and dependability, where partners feel assured of each other's availability and commitment. This trust allows them to seek support, reassurance, and emotional connection without hesitation.
2. **Emotional Intimacy:** People with secure attachment are comfortable sharing their emotions and vulnerabilities, fostering deeper emotional intimacy. This connection is characterized by mutual empathy, understanding, and acceptance.
3. **Autonomy and Interdependence:** Secure attachment balances personal autonomy with interdependence, allowing both partners to maintain individuality while also nurturing the relationship. Both support each other's growth while prioritizing the needs of the partnership.

Strategies for Transitioning to Secure Attachment:

1. **Cultivate Self-Awareness:** Reflect on your attachment style, early caregiver experiences, and behavior patterns in relationships. Understand how past experiences shape your attachment dynamics and identify areas for growth.
2. **Enhance Emotional Regulation:** Develop emotional regulation skills to manage anxiety and fear of vulnerability.

Practice mindfulness, deep breathing, and self-compassion to stay grounded and adaptable.

3. **Foster Open Communication:** Encourage honest conversations about your thoughts, emotions, and needs. Create a space where both partners feel safe to express themselves without fear of judgment or rejection.

4. **Build Trust Through Consistency:** Demonstrate trustworthiness by being reliable and consistent in your words and actions. Fulfill commitments and communicate openly to reinforce trust.

5. **Prioritize Emotional Connection:** Engage in regular conversations, shared experiences, and acts of kindness to nurture the emotional bond. Show appreciation and empathy to deepen your connection.

6. **Seek Support and Growth:** Pursue personal and relational growth through therapy, workshops, or support from trusted individuals. Invest in learning more about attachment dynamics and improving relationship skills.

Building secure attachment requires effort, vulnerability, and a commitment to growing together. By focusing on trust, emotional intimacy, and open communication, couples can strengthen their bond and create a lasting, resilient connection. This transition is an ongoing process that calls for patience, mutual support, and self-compassion.

From Anxious to Secure: Effective Strategies Inspired by Success Stories and Psychological Research

Transitioning from an anxious attachment style to a secure one is a journey that requires self-awareness, emotional growth, and deliberate action. By blending insights from psychological research with the experiences of influential figures, we can identify strategies to facilitate this transformation. Below are step-by-step approaches based on psychological principles and real-life examples to help you move from anxious to secure attachment.

Step 1: Self-Reflection and Awareness Begin by practicing self-reflection to better understand your attachment style and relationship patterns. Reflect on your childhood and early experiences with caregivers to see how they shaped your approach to relationships. Identify the fears, triggers, and behaviors linked to anxious attachment, and recognize their impact on your current relationships.

Example: Oprah Winfrey, the renowned media mogul, openly discusses how self-reflection and therapy helped her heal from childhood trauma and develop emotional resilience. Through self-awareness and personal growth, Oprah transformed her mindset, which contributed to both her personal and professional success.

Step 2: Learn About Attachment Theory Educate yourself on attachment theory and how it influences relationships. Explore the three primary attachment styles—secure, anxious, and avoidant—and how each affects relationship dynamics. Understanding the characteristics and triggers of anxious attachment will help you work toward the healthier, more fulfilling traits of secure attachment.

Example: Kristen Bell, an actress and advocate for mental health awareness, has been candid about her struggles with anxiety and the importance of therapy in improving her emotional well-being and relationships. By learning about attachment theory, Kristen enhanced her personal growth and strengthened her relationships.

Step 3: Challenge Negative Thoughts and Patterns Anxious attachment often stems from fears of abandonment, low self-esteem, and a constant need for reassurance. Cognitive restructuring techniques can help you reframe negative thoughts and develop greater self-compassion, confidence, and emotional resilience. Replace self-doubt with healthier, more constructive beliefs.

Example: Dwayne "The Rock" Johnson overcame childhood challenges and built self-confidence by adopting a positive outlook and consistent self-reflection. His journey of resilience and personal transformation contributed to his success in both his career and personal life.

Step 4: Cultivate Secure Attachment Behaviors Consciously develop habits that promote secure attachment in your relationships. Prioritize open communication, active listening, and empathy to foster emotional closeness and trust. Create a supportive, reliable, and secure relationship dynamic by being consistent and dependable with your partner.

Example: Michelle Obama, former First Lady and best-selling author, exemplifies secure attachment in her marriage to Barack Obama. Their relationship is built on open communication, mutual respect, and shared values, creating a strong foundation of love, trust, and emotional connection.

By applying these strategies, you can gradually transition from anxious to secure attachment, strengthening your emotional well-being and relationships. Remember, this process takes time and effort, but with patience and consistent practice, you can foster healthier, more secure attachments that enrich your life and relationships.

Step 5: Seek Support and Embrace Growth Take advantage of opportunities to grow and seek support from therapy, counseling, or support groups to work through deeper emotional wounds and build stronger relationships. Seeking professional help can guide you on your journey toward secure attachment.

Example: Ryan Reynolds, the Hollywood actor and businessman, has openly discussed his struggles with anxiety and the importance of therapy for his mental health. Through therapy and self-care, Ryan has learned to manage anxiety and improve his mental well-being and relationships.

Step 6: Practice Self-Compassion and Patience Accept that your journey toward secure attachment will have ups and downs. Be kind to yourself and practice self-compassion along the way. Recognize the courage it takes to embrace change and growth.

Example: Lady Gaga, the musician and actress, has been a vocal advocate for mental health and self-acceptance. Her message encourages others to embrace their imperfections and practice self-kindness, promoting resilience through self-love.

By following these transformative strategies, supported by both psychological research and the success stories of influential figures, you can embark on a path toward personal growth, emotional healing, and fulfilling relationships. Remember, change takes time, patience, and persistence, but the rewards of building secure attachments are profound and long-lasting.

Maintaining Your Progress: Tips for Reinforcing New Patterns and Behaviors in the Long Term

Sustaining progress in your shift from anxious to secure attachment requires continued effort and commitment. Here are some tips to help you maintain your progress and foster secure attachment over the long term:

1. **Practice Mindfulness**: Stay present and aware of your thoughts, feelings, and behaviors through mindfulness. It helps you recognize old patterns as they arise, giving you the ability to respond consciously rather than reactively.
2. **Set Boundaries**: Establish and maintain healthy boundaries in your relationships. Clear communication of your needs and limits protects your emotional well-being and reinforces your autonomy.
3. **Engage in Self-Care**: Prioritize activities that nurture your physical, emotional, and mental well-being. Whether it's exercise, hobbies, or spending time with loved ones, self-care ensures you're balanced and fulfilled.
4. **Seek Support**: Surround yourself with supportive individuals, whether friends, family, or a therapist, who provide encouragement and guidance. Share your progress and challenges with people who can validate your experiences.
5. **Challenge Negative Thoughts**: Use cognitive-behavioral techniques to challenge and reframe negative thoughts. Replace self-critical thinking with more realistic, compassionate views.
6. **Celebrate Successes**: Acknowledge your achievements, no matter how small. Celebrating your milestones fosters confidence and motivates you to continue evolving.
7. **Reflect on Your Growth**: Periodically reflect on your personal growth. Whether through journaling, self-reflection, or therapy, take time to gain insights into your progress, assess areas for improvement, and celebrate your positive changes.

By following these steps and maintaining your commitment to growth, you can continue progressing towards secure attachment, cultivating healthier and more fulfilling relationships.

8. Stay Flexible: Be open to feedback, learning, and adaptation on your attachment journey. Flexibility is essential when setbacks arise, as growth often involves overcoming challenges and learning from each experience.

9. Practice Gratitude: Foster a mindset of gratitude by focusing on the positive aspects of your life and relationships. Show appreciation for the progress you've made, the support you've received, and the opportunities for connection and growth ahead.

10. Stay Committed: Continue your commitment to personal growth and emotional well-being, even when obstacles appear. Recognize that change is a gradual process, and each step you take towards secure attachment brings you closer to fulfilling relationships.

By incorporating these strategies into your daily routine, you can reinforce new, healthier patterns that support your journey towards secure attachment. With dedication, self-awareness, and ongoing support, you can sustain your progress and cultivate meaningful relationships based on trust, intimacy, and emotional security.

Practicing Self-Kindness: Nurturing Compassion and Understanding Towards Yourself

Self-kindness means treating yourself with the same compassion and empathy you would offer a close friend or loved one. It's a vital component of self-care and emotional well-being, essential for fostering resilience, self-acceptance, and inner peace. Here are some ways to incorporate self-kindness into your daily life:

1. Cultivate Self-Compassion: Develop a compassionate inner dialogue by speaking kindly to yourself. Acknowledge your humanity, imperfections, and struggles with understanding, rather than self-criticism. Be gentle and supportive toward yourself during challenging times.

2. Practice Self-Care: Make your physical, emotional, and mental well-being a priority. Engage in activities that recharge and nourish you, such as rest, relaxation, hobbies, or spending time with loved ones. Listen to your body's needs and respond with care and attention.

3. Set Realistic Expectations: Be compassionate in setting expectations for yourself. Understand that mistakes and setbacks are part of being human. Focus on progress rather than perfection, and celebrate your efforts and achievements along the way.

By practicing self-kindness, you can cultivate a more nurturing relationship with yourself, one that builds confidence, resilience, and emotional well-being.

4. Forgive Yourself: Let go of the weight of past mistakes or perceived failures by practicing self-forgiveness. Recognize your humanity, learn from your experiences, and release any self-blame or guilt. Each moment offers an opportunity for growth and renewal.

5. Practice Gratitude: Develop gratitude for yourself and your journey by acknowledging your strengths, resilience, and innate worthiness. Take time to appreciate your efforts, achievements, and the qualities that make you unique and valuable.

6. Set Boundaries: Respect your needs and boundaries with kindness and assertiveness, ensuring that your well-being is a priority in all relationships. Practice saying no when necessary, and communicate your limits with compassion and clarity.

7. Seek Support: Reach out to trusted friends, family, or professionals for encouragement, guidance, or validation. Be open to receiving love and support, knowing that you deserve care and compassion from others.

8. Practice Mindfulness: Engage in mindfulness practices to embrace present-moment awareness with non-judgmental acceptance of your thoughts and feelings. Approach your experiences with curiosity and openness, showing kindness towards yourself in every moment.

9. Celebrate Your Successes: Celebrate all your achievements, whether big or small, as milestones of your efforts, growth, and adaptability. Take pride in your journey and recognize the progress you've made in nurturing self-compassion and well-being.

10. Be Your Own Cheerleader: Offer yourself encouragement, affirmation, and support, especially during challenging times.

Remind yourself of your strengths and inherent worth, believing in your capacity to navigate life's challenges with grace and resilience.

By practicing self-kindness consistently, you can foster a greater sense of self-acceptance, emotional resilience, and inner peace, laying the foundation for a fulfilling and balanced life.

Overcoming Self-Criticism: Embracing Compassion and Self-Acceptance

Overcoming self-criticism involves replacing negative self-talk with compassion and fostering self-acceptance. Self-criticism, often rooted in internalized judgments and unrealistic standards, can erode self-esteem and hinder growth. Here are effective strategies to help you move past self-criticism and build a more compassionate and accepting relationship with yourself:

1. Practice Self-Compassion: Replace self-criticism with self-compassion by treating yourself with the same kindness and understanding you would offer a close friend. Acknowledge your humanity, imperfections, and inherent worth, offering empathy and support during difficult moments.

2. Challenge Negative Thoughts: Recognize and challenge the validity of negative self-talk. Question whether these self-critical thoughts are based on truth or are rooted in unrealistic expectations. Replace them with more balanced, kind, and compassionate perspectives.

3. Cultivate Self-Awareness: Pay attention to your inner dialogue and recognize when self-criticism arises. Approach these thoughts with curiosity rather than judgment, seeking to understand their origins, triggers, and impact on your well-being. By becoming aware, you can begin to disrupt the cycle of negativity.

4. Practice Gratitude: Focus on gratitude by acknowledging your strengths, accomplishments, and the positive aspects of your life. Express appreciation for your efforts and uniqueness, fostering a mindset of abundance rather than focusing solely on perceived shortcomings.

5. Celebrate Progress: Acknowledge and celebrate your progress, no matter how small. Understand that personal growth is a gradual process, requiring patience and resilience. Celebrate each achievement, step forward, or learning experience with kindness, encouraging yourself to keep moving forward.

By adopting these strategies, you can gradually overcome self-criticism, cultivate self-compassion, and foster a greater sense of self-acceptance, leading to enhanced well-being and personal growth.

6. Set Realistic Expectations: Create goals that align with your abilities, recognizing both your strengths and limitations. Avoid comparing yourself to others or striving for perfection, and focus on growth and progress, appreciating small wins and learning experiences along the way.

7. Practice Self-Care: Prioritize activities that nourish your mind, body, and spirit. Engage in regular exercise, enjoy moments of relaxation, and invest time in creative expression or being in nature. Listening to your needs and taking time to recharge will help you maintain balance and well-being.

8. Seek Support: Reach out to friends, family, or professionals when you need encouragement or guidance. Sharing your struggles with those who offer empathy and perspective helps reduce isolation and allows you to gain strength from their support.

9. Forgive Yourself: Let go of past mistakes and regrets by practicing self-forgiveness. Recognize that imperfection is part of the human experience, and view mistakes as opportunities for growth. Be kind to yourself as you move forward with a lighter heart.

10. Embrace Imperfection: Accept your imperfections and vulnerabilities as integral parts of who you are. Celebrate the beauty of authenticity and adaptability, and honor your unique qualities. Embracing imperfection allows you to live more freely and wholeheartedly.

By incorporating these strategies into your life, you can slowly shift away from self-criticism and embrace self-compassion, acceptance, and emotional resilience. Remember, self-acceptance is a continuous journey, and each step toward treating yourself with kindness and understanding contributes to a more authentic and fulfilling life.

Expanding Secure Attachment Beyond Romance: Nurturing Healthy Relationships in All Areas of Life

Secure attachment isn't limited to romantic relationships. It forms the foundation for healthy connections across various areas of life, promoting emotional well-being, fulfillment, and resilience. Here's how you can nurture secure attachment in different types of relationships:

1. Family Relationships:
Encourage secure attachment within your family by fostering open communication, mutual respect, and emotional support. Spend quality time together, express gratitude for one another, and work through conflicts constructively to strengthen the familial bond.

2. Friendships:
Develop secure attachments with friends by being dependable, honest, and supportive. Practice active listening, show empathy, and provide validation in your friendships. Invest in meaningful connections with friends who enrich and support you.

3. Professional Relationships:
In the workplace, foster secure attachment by building trust, respect, and collaboration with colleagues. Communicate openly, offer and accept constructive feedback, and contribute to a positive work environment that nurtures emotional security and professional growth.

4. Community Involvement:
Engage in community activities that promote a sense of belonging and contribution. Whether through volunteering, joining clubs, or attending local events, cultivating secure attachments within your community connects you with others who share your values and interests.

5. Mentorship and Guidance:
Seek out mentors who can offer guidance and encouragement. Build secure attachments by respecting their wisdom and maintaining

open, honest communication. Mentorship relationships thrive when based on mutual trust and learning.

6. Self-Attachment:
Foster a secure attachment with yourself by practicing self-compassion, self-care, and self-awareness. Cultivate a kind and supportive inner dialogue, honor your needs, and embrace your individuality. Treat yourself with the same love and respect you offer others.

7. Pet Relationships:
Build secure attachments with pets by providing love, care, and companionship. Pets offer unconditional love and emotional support, helping you experience security, comfort, and joy.

8. Hobbies and Interests:
Engage in hobbies or creative pursuits that bring you fulfillment and a sense of purpose. These activities can connect you with like-minded individuals, fostering a sense of community and belonging while deepening your attachment to meaningful interests.

9. Spiritual Connections:
Cultivate secure attachment through spiritual practices or beliefs that provide a deeper sense of meaning and connection. Whether through meditation, faith communities, or spiritual retreats, engaging in spiritual practices can offer profound emotional support and grounding.

10. Personal Growth and Development:
Invest in your personal growth through therapy, coaching, or self-development resources. Cultivating secure attachment within yourself requires ongoing self-reflection, emotional resilience, and a commitment to overcoming hurdles and nurturing self-worth.

By extending secure attachment principles beyond romantic partnerships, you can strengthen your sense of connection, emotional stability, and overall well-being in every aspect of your life. Remember, secure attachment is a journey that continues to grow with intention and mindful nurturing.

Key Takeaways:

- **Understanding Secure Attachment:** This chapter provides a clear overview of secure attachment, highlighting its characteristics such as trust, emotional openness, and a sense of security. Readers will explore how secure attachment fosters stable and healthy intimate relationships.
- **Building Trust:** Trust is the cornerstone of secure attachment. The chapter outlines strategies to build trust through consistent communication, reliability, and mutual respect, helping create a stable foundation for relationships.
- **Embracing Vulnerability:** Vulnerability is vital for deepening intimacy. The chapter emphasizes the importance of vulnerability in expressing authenticity, fostering emotional closeness, and strengthening trust with a partner.
- **Effective Communication:** Secure attachment relies on open, honest communication. Readers will gain practical communication skills like active listening, empathy, and assertiveness to promote understanding, validation, and emotional responsiveness.
- **Setting Boundaries:** Boundaries are crucial for maintaining individuality and well-being. The chapter discusses how setting and respecting boundaries enhances autonomy, mutual respect, and emotional safety in relationships.
- **Healing from Past Wounds:** Individuals with anxious attachment may need to heal from past trauma to move toward secure attachment. Techniques such as inner child work, trauma processing, and self-compassion practices are explored to facilitate healing and resilience.
- **Cultivating Connection:** Secure attachment thrives on deep connection and intimacy. Strategies are provided for nurturing connection through shared experiences, emotional attunement, and acts of kindness and appreciation.

Action Steps/Call to Action:

- Reflect on your attachment patterns and identify areas where you can grow towards secure attachment.
- Practice building trust and embracing vulnerability through open communication and emotional honesty in your relationships.

Stay tuned for the next chapter, where practical exercises and strategies for cultivating secure attachment will be explored, fostering greater trust, vulnerability, and connection in your relationships.

Chapter 9:

Developing Emotional Regulation Abilities

Triggers are stimuli or events that provoke strong emotional reactions due to past experiences, often tied to trauma, stress, or unresolved emotional pain. Learning to recognize and manage triggers is crucial for maintaining emotional balance and developing healthy coping mechanisms. Here's how to approach managing triggers with self-awareness and flexibility:

1. **Recognize Your Triggers**: Take time to pinpoint specific situations, events, or interactions that lead to intense emotional responses. Reflect on past patterns and experiences that commonly lead to feelings like anxiety, anger, sadness, or fear.

2. **Observe Physical and Emotional Signals**: Pay attention to the physical sensations and emotional signals that accompany your trigger responses, such as a rapid heartbeat, shallow breathing, muscle tension, or overwhelming thoughts. Recognizing these early signs can help you catch the trigger before it escalates.

3. **Examine Root Causes**: Delve into the deeper emotions and beliefs underlying your trigger reactions. Consider which past experiences or core beliefs may be fueling your current emotional responses, and how they shape your reactions.

4. **Practice Mindfulness**: Engage in mindfulness practices to observe your thoughts, feelings, and bodily sensations without judgment. Techniques like mindfulness meditation, deep breathing, or body scans help ground you in the present, creating space between the trigger and your response.

5. **Build Coping Tools**: Develop a set of coping strategies that help you handle trigger responses effectively. These may include relaxation exercises, grounding techniques, visualization, or activities that soothe and stabilize your emotions.

6. **Set Clear Boundaries**: Establish personal boundaries to limit your exposure to triggering situations where possible. Assertively communicate your needs and limits, and create

safe spaces where you can withdraw when triggered to regain emotional balance.

7. **Seek Support**: Reach out to trusted friends, family, or mental health professionals when triggers feel too overwhelming. Sharing your experiences with supportive individuals can provide empathy, validation, and new perspectives to help you manage your emotions.

8. **Practice Self-Compassion**: Be kind and understanding towards yourself when faced with triggers. Recognize that your reactions are normal responses to past emotional wounds. Offer yourself encouragement and avoid blaming or judging yourself for how you feel.

9. **Process Emotions in Healthy Ways**: Find constructive outlets to process your emotions when triggered. Journaling, creative activities, or therapy can help you explore your feelings, release emotional tension, and gain a deeper understanding of your triggers, promoting emotional healing.

10. **Develop a Self-Care Routine**: Create a self-care plan that prioritizes your well-being. Incorporate practices like exercise, proper nutrition, sufficient rest, and activities that bring joy and relaxation into your daily life to maintain emotional balance.

By approaching triggers with awareness, flexibility, and self-compassion, you can manage your emotional reactions more effectively and achieve greater emotional stability. Healing from triggers is a gradual process, so remember to be patient with yourself and prioritize self-care as part of your journey toward emotional well-being.

Techniques for Emotional Regulation: Cultivating Balance and Adaptability

Emotional regulation is the ability to manage and adjust emotions in healthy ways, promoting emotional balance and resilience. Developing these techniques can help individuals handle emotional challenges and enhance their overall well-being. Below are some strategies for effective emotional regulation:

1. **Deep Breathing**: Engage in deep breathing exercises to trigger the body's relaxation response and soothe the nervous system. Breathe deeply through your nose, expanding your

abdomen, and exhale slowly through your mouth, releasing tension and stress with each breath.

2. **Mindfulness Meditation**: Practice mindfulness meditation to increase awareness of the present moment without judgment. This allows you to observe your emotions with curiosity and acceptance, helping you process feelings without becoming overwhelmed by them.

3. **Progressive Muscle Relaxation**: Systematically tense and relax each muscle group in your body, starting from your feet and moving up to your head. This technique helps release physical tension, promoting relaxation and emotional calmness.

4. **Grounding Techniques**: Focus on your immediate environment to center yourself and reduce feelings of anxiety or distress. Engage your senses by noticing sights, sounds, smells, textures, and tastes around you, bringing your attention back to the present moment.

5. **Self-Soothing Activities**: Participate in activities that offer comfort and relaxation, such as taking a warm bath, listening to soothing music, or engaging in hobbies that bring joy. Self-soothing promotes emotional balance during stressful times.

6. **Emotion Labeling**: Identify and name your emotions to help make sense of your emotional experiences. By saying "I feel frustrated" or "I'm feeling sad," you acknowledge and validate your emotions, making it easier to regulate them.

7. **Cognitive Restructuring**: Challenge negative or distorted thoughts that fuel emotional distress. Recognize irrational beliefs or cognitive distortions, like all-or-nothing thinking, and replace them with more realistic, balanced perspectives.

By incorporating these emotional regulation techniques into daily life, you can foster adaptability, manage emotional triggers effectively, and maintain a greater sense of emotional well-being.

8. Social Support: Reach out to trusted friends, family, or mental health professionals when managing emotions feels overwhelming. Sharing your experiences with people who can offer empathy, understanding, and advice can help you feel validated and supported.

9. Physical Activity: Regular exercise is an effective way to release built-up tension, improve mood through the release of endorphins, and promote mental well-being. Choose activities that you enjoy and that suit your fitness level to make physical activity a regular, positive part of your emotional regulation toolkit.

10. Journaling: Keeping a journal allows you to express and process emotions by writing freely about your thoughts and feelings. Journaling helps you reflect on your emotional experiences with honesty, which can provide insights and promote self-compassion.

Incorporating these techniques into your routine can significantly enhance your emotional regulation, helping you cope better with stress and challenges while building emotional resilience. Find the strategies that work best for you, and remember that emotional regulation is a skill that improves over time with consistent practice and patience.

Cultivating Presence, Awareness, and Inner Peace

Mindfulness and meditation are transformative practices rooted in ancient traditions like Buddhism and Taoism, known for promoting inner peace, emotional balance, and mental well-being. In recent years, these practices have gained global recognition for their proven benefits on mental, emotional, and physical health. In this section, we'll dive into the core principles of mindfulness and meditation, explore their benefits, and learn how to apply them practically in everyday life.

Exploring Mindfulness

Mindfulness is the art of bringing intentional, non-judgmental awareness to the present moment. It encourages an open and curious attitude toward our thoughts, feelings, bodily sensations, and surroundings. Rather than reacting impulsively to stressors, mindfulness teaches us to observe our experiences without getting entangled in them. This practice fosters clarity and emotional balance, allowing us to navigate life's challenges with enhanced adaptability, patience, and inner calm.

Here are the benefits listed:

1. Reduced Stress
2. Improved Sleep
3. Relieves Anxiety

4. Increases Empathy
5. Improved Self-Esteem
6. Boosts Focus
7. Reduces Depression
8. Improved Awareness
9. Increases Energy
10. Improved Mood

These benefits highlight mindfulness as a powerful tool for enhancing mental, emotional, and physical well-being. The overall design uses nature-themed elements, suggesting a connection between mindfulness and inner peace, harmony, and balance.

Mindfulness offers numerous well-documented benefits for overall well-being. Below is an expanded list of the key advantages:

1. **Stress Reduction**: By encouraging relaxation and helping calm the nervous system, mindfulness reduces stress, leading to a greater sense of peace and inner balance.
2. **Emotional Regulation**: Mindfulness enhances our ability to manage emotions by increasing awareness of our internal states. This leads to more adaptive and composed responses in difficult situations.
3. **Improved Focus and Concentration**: Regular mindfulness practice improves cognitive abilities and enhances attention control, making it easier to stay present and focused in day-to-day tasks.
4. **Enhanced Self-Awareness**: Mindfulness encourages self-reflection, enabling us to better understand our thoughts, emotions, and behavioral patterns. This insight fosters personal growth and self-discovery.
5. **Greater Compassion and Empathy**: Mindfulness nurtures a sense of kindness and compassion toward ourselves and others. It enhances emotional connections and encourages healthier, more supportive relationships.
6. **Pain Management**: Research shows that mindfulness helps reduce chronic pain and improve pain tolerance by altering how the brain perceives and processes pain signals.

These benefits reflect mindfulness' ability to promote mental clarity, emotional resilience, and physical comfort, supporting a balanced and harmonious life.

Incorporating mindfulness into daily life can significantly improve mental, emotional, and physical well-being. Below are practical techniques for cultivating mindfulness:

1. **Mindful Breathing**: Spend a few moments focusing on your breath, paying attention to the sensations of each inhale and exhale. Notice how your abdomen rises and falls or how the air feels as it moves in and out of your nostrils, helping you ground in the present.
2. **Body Scan Meditation**: Either lying down or sitting comfortably, bring your awareness to different parts of your body, starting from your toes and moving toward your head. Acknowledge any sensations or tension without judgment, allowing relaxation to release any stress.
3. **Mindful Eating**: Slow down during meals, savoring each bite by paying attention to the food's colors, textures, flavors, and smells. Chew deliberately, observing how your body responds to the nourishment, encouraging appreciation and presence.
4. **Walking Meditation**: As you walk, focus on the sensations of each step and the movement in your body. Pay attention to your surroundings—the sights, sounds, and smells—grounding yourself in the present moment as you walk.
5. **Mindful Listening**: Engage in conversations with full attention, practicing active listening. Avoid interrupting or formulating responses while the other person speaks. Notice their tone, body language, and emotions, fostering empathy and deeper connections.
6. **Mindful Movement**: Participate in activities like yoga, tai chi, or qigong with full awareness of the sensations in your body, your breath, and energy flow. Move with intention and mindfulness, creating a harmonious connection between body and mind.

By practicing these mindfulness techniques, you can foster greater self-awareness, presence, and emotional balance throughout your day.

"Opportunities for Mindfulness in Daily Life"through simple, everyday activities.

These moments can be used to practice mindfulness, helping to cultivate presence and awareness. The activities featured include:

1. **Brushing Your Teeth**: Focus on the sensations of brushing, the feel of the toothbrush, and the taste of the toothpaste.
2. **Driving in Silence or with Calming Music**: Use the drive as a time to focus on the road, your breath, and your surroundings, or enjoy calming music to center yourself.
3. **Doing the Dishes or Laundry**: Engage fully in the act of washing dishes or handling laundry, paying attention to the tactile sensations, sounds, and movements involved.
4. **Relaxing with Kids While Getting Them Ready for Bed**: Be fully present with your children, enjoying the moment without distractions, and connecting through the bedtime routine.
5. **Exercising Without Music or TV, Focusing on Breathing Instead**: Focus on your breath and body movement during exercise to deepen your connection with the present moment.

These simple, routine moments offer valuable opportunities to integrate mindfulness into daily life, helping to bring a sense of calm and presence into everyday activities.

Understanding Meditation: Meditation is a practice that involves training the mind to reach a state of heightened focus, awareness, and inner peace. It helps individuals cultivate mental clarity, emotional stability, and spiritual insight through various techniques and approaches. Some common forms of meditation include:

1. **Concentration Meditation**: Focuses attention on a single point, such as the breath, a candle flame, or a mantra, to train the mind to maintain focus and prevent distraction.
2. **Mindfulness Meditation**: Involves observing thoughts, emotions, and sensations without judgment, cultivating a non-reactive awareness of the present moment.
3. **Loving-Kindness Meditation (Metta)**: Aims to develop feelings of compassion, love, and goodwill towards oneself and others, often using phrases like "May I be happy, may I be well."

4. **Transcendental Meditation**: Involves silently repeating a mantra to transcend ordinary thought and enter a deep state of restful alertness.

While mindfulness is a popular form of meditation, the broader spectrum of meditation practices is geared towards enhancing self-awareness, emotional regulation, and mental and spiritual well-being.

Benefits of Meditation: Meditation provides a wide range of benefits for mental, emotional, and physical well-being. Key advantages include:

1. **Reduced Anxiety and Depression**: Meditation helps alleviate anxiety and depression by encouraging relaxation, improving emotional regulation, and fostering a positive mindset.
2. **Enhanced Cognitive Function**: Regular meditation enhances cognitive abilities, including memory, attention, and problem-solving, leading to clearer thinking and improved focus.
3. **Stress Management**: Meditation reduces stress by triggering the body's relaxation response, lowering cortisol (the stress hormone), and promoting a sense of calm and peace.
4. **Improved Sleep Quality**: Meditation improves sleep by calming the mind, reducing insomnia, and facilitating deeper, more restful sleep.
5. **Emotional Adaptability**: Through increased self-awareness and emotional balance, meditation helps people navigate life's challenges with more resilience, equanimity, and emotional flexibility.
6. **Enhanced Well-Being**: Meditation promotes inner peace, a sense of contentment, and a deeper connection with oneself and the broader world, contributing to overall well-being and fulfillment.

These benefits make meditation a powerful tool for improving both mental health and emotional adaptability, as well as enhancing daily life.

Practical Meditation Techniques:

1. **Focused Attention Meditation**:
   o Focus your attention on a single point, such as your breath, a candle flame, or a specific mantra. When your mind wanders, gently bring it back to the chosen focal point without judgment. This practice helps improve concentration and mental clarity.
2. **Mindfulness Meditation**:
   o Sit quietly and observe your thoughts, emotions, and sensations as they arise without trying to change them. Acknowledge them with curiosity and non-judgment, allowing them to pass naturally. This promotes self-awareness and emotional balance.
3. **Loving-Kindness Meditation (Metta)**:
   o Begin by cultivating feelings of love and kindness towards yourself, then extend those feelings to others, including friends, family, and even difficult individuals. Repeat phrases like "May I be happy. May you be happy," to foster compassion and empathy.
4. **Body Scan Meditation**:
   o Lie down or sit comfortably and slowly direct your attention to each part of your body, starting from your toes and moving upward. Notice any sensations or tension and allow your body to relax deeply. This practice enhances body awareness and promotes relaxation.
5. **Guided Visualization**:
   o Follow a guided meditation, either through an app or recording, where you visualize calming and peaceful scenes like walking in a forest or sitting by the ocean. This technique reduces stress and helps create a sense of peace and calm.
6. **Transcendental Meditation**:
   o In this practice, silently repeat a specific mantra for 15-20 minutes, twice a day. The repetition of the mantra helps the mind settle into a state of restful awareness. This method enhances relaxation, creativity, and overall well-being.
7. **Walking Meditation**:
   o Take slow, deliberate steps, focusing on the sensation of each step as your foot touches the ground. Pay attention to your breath, the movement of your body, and the environment around you. This technique is a

great way to incorporate mindfulness into physical activity.

8. **Breathing Meditation (Pranayama)**:
   o Focus on your breath by inhaling slowly and deeply through your nose, holding for a few seconds, then exhaling slowly through your mouth. Various breathing patterns can be used to regulate energy and emotional states. This helps balance the mind and body, reducing anxiety and enhancing focus.

Incorporating these practical meditation techniques into your daily routine can promote greater mental clarity, emotional resilience, and a profound sense of peace and well-being. Experiment with different styles to find what resonates with you most.

Incorporating Mindfulness and Meditation into Daily Life:

Integrating mindfulness and meditation into your routine can significantly enhance your overall well-being. Here are some practical tips for making these practices part of your daily life:

1. **Set Aside Time for Practice**:
   o Dedicate a specific time each day for mindfulness or meditation. Whether it's in the morning to start your day with clarity, during lunch to reset, or before bed to unwind, consistency is key. Start with just a few minutes and gradually extend the duration as you grow more comfortable.
2. **Create a Sacred Space**:
   o Designate a quiet, comfortable area free from distractions for your practice. Add calming elements like candles, cushions, or plants to make the space feel inviting and serene. This can serve as a sanctuary for daily reflection and contemplation.
3. **Start Small**:
   o If you're new to mindfulness or meditation, begin with short, manageable sessions focusing on one technique at a time. Whether it's deep breathing or body scan meditation, experiment with different methods to discover what resonates best for you.
4. **Be Consistent**:

o Regular practice is essential for experiencing the full benefits of mindfulness and meditation. Even on days when you feel distracted or resistant, commit to showing up. Each practice session, no matter how brief, contributes to your personal growth and mental clarity.

5. **Practice Informal Mindfulness**:
   o Incorporate mindfulness into your everyday activities. Whether eating, walking, or doing household tasks like washing dishes, bring your full attention to the sensations, sounds, and movements involved. This simple shift in awareness can make routine tasks more mindful and meaningful.

6. **Be Gentle with Yourself**:
   o Approach mindfulness and meditation with patience, gentleness, and self-compassion. There's no need for perfection. Let go of judgment, and allow yourself to be present with whatever arises in the moment, embracing curiosity and acceptance.

7. **Seek Guidance and Support**:
   o Explore mindfulness and meditation through books, apps, or online resources. Attend workshops, classes, or retreats for deeper insight and community support. Learning from experienced teachers can inspire your practice and offer valuable tools to further your progress.

Mindfulness and meditation have the potential to transform your mental, emotional, and physical health. By consistently cultivating presence, awareness, and inner peace, you can navigate life's challenges with greater resilience and clarity. Whether your goal is stress relief, emotional balance, or spiritual growth, mindfulness and meditation provide practical tools for enriching your life. Start incorporating them today and discover their profound benefits.

Friendships and Family: Applying Principles of Secure Attachment to Other Important Relationships in Your Life

Just as secure attachment is essential in romantic relationships, it plays a crucial role in nurturing healthy and supportive friendships and family connections. By applying the principles of secure attachment to these relationships, you can build stronger bonds, foster trust, and create emotional safety. Here's how to cultivate secure attachments in friendships and family relationships:

1. **Open Communication**:
   - Encourage open, honest dialogue in your friendships and family relationships. Share your thoughts, feelings, and needs openly and listen to others without judgment. Express empathy and validation to strengthen mutual understanding and trust, making others feel heard and valued.

2. **Consistency and Reliability**:
   - Be dependable and reliable in your interactions with friends and family members. Show up consistently, keep your promises, and follow through on commitments. This builds a foundation of trust and predictability, fostering emotional security in your relationships.

3. **Emotional Support**:
   - Offer emotional support when friends or family members are going through challenges. Be present, provide a listening ear, and validate their emotions. Whether it's through advice, practical help, or simply being there, your support deepens the emotional connection and trust.

4. **Boundaries and Autonomy**:
   - Respect personal boundaries and each individual's need for autonomy in your relationships. Honor differences, allow personal space, and recognize that healthy relationships involve mutual respect for each other's individuality. This promotes a balanced sense of connection and independence.

5. **Conflict Resolution**:
   - Address conflicts with empathy and understanding. When disagreements arise, approach the situation calmly and listen to the other person's perspective. Use assertive communication, active listening, and compromise to resolve conflicts constructively, which strengthens the bond and encourages secure attachment.

6. **Quality Time Together**:
   - Prioritize spending quality time with friends and family. Engage in shared activities, conversations, or simple moments that bring you closer and foster

feelings of connection. Quality time enhances emotional intimacy and solidifies your sense of belonging in these relationships.

7. **Celebrate Achievements**:
    o Celebrate the accomplishments and milestones of your friends and family members. Whether big or small, acknowledge and support their achievements with encouragement and genuine happiness. This not only boosts their confidence but also reinforces a positive and loving connection.

By embracing these secure attachment principles in your friendships and family relationships, you can nurture deeper emotional bonds, foster trust, and provide mutual support. These healthy relationships enrich your life with love, security, and a strong sense of belonging, creating a solid network of meaningful connections.

Building a Support Network: Advice on Seeking Out and Promoting Supportive Communities

Building a strong support network is key to emotional resilience, personal growth, and overall well-being. Supportive communities provide encouragement, understanding, and practical help during life's challenges. Here's how to seek out and nurture supportive networks:

1. **Identify Your Needs**:
    o Reflect on the kind of support you need—whether it's emotional, social, or practical. Identifying these needs helps you focus on where to seek connections and support, whether it's in your personal life, professional development, or specific life challenges.
2. **Reach Out to Existing Relationships**:
    o Strengthen relationships with friends, family, and colleagues who already play a role in your support system. Foster these relationships through open communication, mutual respect, and reciprocity. Deepening existing connections can enhance your sense of belonging and emotional support.
3. **Join Community Groups**:
    o Look for local or online community groups, clubs, or organizations that match your interests, values, or

hobbies. Whether it's a book club, hiking group, or a professional organization, these groups provide shared experiences, friendships, and opportunities for meaningful connections.

4. **Attend Support Groups**:
   o Consider joining support groups focused on specific life challenges, such as mental health, addiction recovery, grief, or caregiving. These groups offer a non-judgmental space to share experiences, receive empathy, and gain insights from people facing similar struggles.

5. **Volunteer or Get Involved**:
   o Volunteering allows you to connect with others while contributing to causes you care about. Whether it's community service, charity work, or local events, volunteering builds camaraderie, deepens your sense of purpose, and introduces you to supportive individuals.

6. **Utilize Online Communities**:
   o Seek out online communities, forums, or social media groups centered around your interests or experiences. These virtual spaces offer a platform to share advice, seek support, and connect with individuals worldwide who understand and relate to your journey.

7. **Be Vulnerable and Authentic**:
   o Foster genuine connections by practicing vulnerability and authenticity. Share your real thoughts and feelings without fear of judgment. By being open and honest, you'll create deeper, more trusting relationships within your support network.

8. **Offer Support to Others**:
   o Support is reciprocal. Be proactive in offering help, encouragement, and empathy to others in your community. By cultivating a spirit of giving, you contribute to a culture of mutual care and strengthen the overall bond within the group.

9. **Maintain Boundaries**:
   o Set healthy boundaries to protect your emotional well-being. It's essential to balance supporting others with taking care of yourself. Prioritize self-care and avoid taking on too much responsibility within your network to prevent burnout.

10. **Stay Open to New Connections**:

- Be open-minded and welcoming to forming new relationships. As you meet new people, stay curious about their perspectives, experiences, and backgrounds. Your support network will naturally expand as you remain open to new, diverse connections.

By seeking out and building a supportive community, you'll create a network of relationships that uplift and empower you. This ongoing process of mutual care and connection will help you navigate life's challenges with adaptability, compassion, and resilience.

Key Takeaways:

• **Understanding Emotional Regulation**: This chapter introduces the concept of emotional regulation and its significance in maintaining both mental health and positive relationships. It explores how emotional regulation helps individuals manage stress, resolve conflicts, and build healthier connections with others.

• **Identifying Triggers**: Recognizing emotional triggers is the first step in developing emotional regulation. Readers will learn how to identify specific situations, thoughts, or events that cause heightened emotional reactions, enabling them to take proactive steps in managing their responses.

• **Mindfulness Practices**: Mindfulness techniques, such as deep breathing, meditation, and body scanning, are key tools for emotional regulation. This chapter covers how these practices can increase awareness of thoughts and emotions, helping individuals respond more skillfully to stress and emotional challenges.

• **Cognitive Restructuring**: Cognitive restructuring involves transforming negative or distorted thinking patterns that lead to emotional dysregulation. Readers will discover cognitive-behavioral techniques such as reframing and challenging irrational thoughts to foster healthier thinking patterns and emotional balance.

• **Stress Management Techniques**: Emotional regulation often falters under stress. This chapter provides stress management strategies, including relaxation techniques, time management, and physical activity, which help reduce stress levels and maintain emotional stability.

• **Emotion Regulation Strategies**: Readers will gain insights into various emotion regulation strategies like emotion labeling, expressive writing, and visualization. These techniques support emotional awareness and help manage strong emotions with resilience and calmness.

• **Seeking Support**: Emotional regulation is often easier with the support of others. The chapter emphasizes the importance of seeking help from trusted friends, family, or professionals for guidance, encouragement, and accountability as readers work towards emotional well-being.

Action Steps/Call to Action: • Reflect on your current emotional regulation abilities and identify areas where you could improve. • Incorporate mindfulness and stress management practices into your daily routine to build emotional awareness and resilience.

Stay engaged for the next chapter, where we will explore practical exercises for *"Rewriting Internal Narratives"* and strategies for building emotional regulation skills, fostering greater stability, and promoting well-being in your relationships and life. Through actionable steps and insights, you'll learn how to reshape limiting beliefs, strengthen emotional resilience, and cultivate healthier patterns for long-lasting positive change.

Chapter 10:
Transforming Inner Narratives

Negative beliefs are ingrained patterns of thought that can stifle potential, erode confidence, and hinder personal progress. Often rooted in past experiences, cultural influences, or internalized messages, these beliefs shape how we view ourselves and the world. Challenging and transforming them is key to personal growth, emotional well-being, and goal achievement. Here's how to break free from limiting thoughts and behaviors:

1. **Identify Negative Beliefs**: Begin by recognizing the negative beliefs that hold you back. Pay attention to recurring self-doubts or critical thoughts that harm your confidence. Common beliefs might include "I'm not good enough," "I don't deserve success," or "I'll never change."

2. **Examine the Evidence**: Challenge these beliefs by evaluating the facts. Ask yourself if there's substantial evidence supporting these thoughts or if they're based on assumptions, distortions, or past experiences. Explore alternate viewpoints that counter these negative narratives.

3. **Question Distorted Thinking**: Learn to spot and question cognitive distortions that fuel negative beliefs. These might include black-and-white thinking, catastrophizing, over-generalizing, or taking things personally. Replace negative thoughts with more balanced, realistic, and compassionate perspectives.

4. **Explore Origins and Triggers**: Reflect on where your negative beliefs originated and what triggers them. Think about past experiences, relationships, or societal messages that may have shaped these beliefs. Identify the situations or contexts that activate these self-limiting patterns.

5. **Practice Self-Compassion**: Nurture self-compassion as you work through your negative beliefs. Treat yourself with the empathy and kindness you'd extend to a friend going through similar challenges. Embrace your inherent worth, independent of any perceived shortcomings or mistakes.

6. **Challenge Perfectionism**: Confront the belief that perfection is necessary for success or self-worth. Accept that imperfection is part of the human experience and offers opportunities for growth. Set achievable, realistic goals, and

recognize that progress, not perfection, is what matters. Celebrate your steps forward, no matter how small.

7. **Seek Counterexamples**: Actively look for examples that disprove your negative beliefs. Reflect on past achievements, skills, and strengths that highlight your abilities and growth. Remind yourself of times when you overcame challenges, proving your adaptability and competence.

8. **Practice Affirmations**: Use affirmations to rewire your mindset and reinforce a positive self-image. Repeat empowering statements that affirm your worth, potential, and resilience. Choose phrases that personally resonate with you, helping you internalize the positive qualities you want to strengthen.

9. **Challenge Core Beliefs**: Address the deep-rooted beliefs that drive multiple negative thoughts and behaviors. Examine the fears or insecurities that underpin these beliefs and entertain new, healthier perspectives. Cognitive restructuring can help you reshape these core beliefs, leading to more constructive thinking.

10. **Take Action**: Begin taking small, intentional steps to counteract negative beliefs and boost your self-confidence. Set realistic, attainable goals aligned with your values and take action that contradicts your self-doubts. These efforts will reinforce a sense of accomplishment and self-efficacy.

By consistently challenging and reframing negative beliefs, you can foster a more empowering outlook on life. As you replace self-limiting thoughts with realistic, positive perspectives, you'll cultivate confidence, adaptability, and a more meaningful life. The process of transforming negative beliefs is gradual—approach it with patience, persistence, and kindness toward yourself, celebrating each milestone along the way.

Cognitive Restructuring Exercises: Rewiring Your Thought Patterns for Positive Change

Cognitive restructuring is a key technique in cognitive-behavioral therapy (CBT) that helps challenge and shift negative thought patterns into more balanced and adaptive ways of thinking. By addressing these distorted thoughts, individuals can improve their mood, develop emotional adaptability, and enhance overall well-being. Here are some cognitive restructuring exercises to help you rewire your thought patterns for positive change:

1. **Identifying Automatic Thoughts**:
   Start by recognizing automatic thoughts—those quick, spontaneous thoughts that arise in response to certain situations. Keeping a thought diary or journal can help track these thoughts as they occur throughout the day. Identify recurring themes in your thinking.
   Exercise: Reflect on a recent stressful event. Jot down the automatic thoughts that came to mind without filtering or judging them.
   Example: "I'll never be able to do this," "I always mess things up," "Nobody cares about me."

2. **Examining Evidence**:
   Once you've identified your automatic thoughts, evaluate the evidence supporting or refuting them. Ask: What objective evidence supports this thought? Is there evidence that contradicts it? Consider alternative interpretations.
   Exercise: Choose one automatic thought and examine the evidence for and against it. Write down both.
   Example: "I made a mistake at work, so I'll never succeed" (Supporting evidence: "I did make a mistake." Contradicting evidence: "I've succeeded in other tasks before.").

3. **Considering Worst-Case Scenarios**:
   Challenge catastrophic thinking by evaluating the worst-case scenario. Ask: What's the worst that could happen? How likely is it? How would I cope if it happened? This helps reduce anxiety by putting situations into perspective.
   Exercise: Identify a recent anxiety-provoking thought and assess its worst-case scenario. Evaluate its likelihood and consider what you'd do if it happened.
   Example: "If I fail this project, my career is over." (Likelihood: Unlikely. What I'd do: Learn from the experience, improve, and try again.)

4. **Identifying Thinking Errors**:
   Learn to recognize common thinking errors, such as black-and-white thinking, over-generalization, and personalization. Once you notice these distortions, reframe them with more balanced and realistic perspectives.
   Exercise: Identify a thinking error in a recent automatic thought. Write down a balanced perspective to counteract it.
   Example: "I failed this time, so I'm a total failure" (Black-

and-white thinking). Balanced perspective: "Making mistakes is part of learning and growing; it doesn't define my worth as a person."

5. **Reframing Negative Thoughts**:
Reframe your negative thoughts by considering alternative viewpoints. Ask: What's a more constructive or neutral way to interpret this situation?
Exercise: Take a negative thought and reframe it into a positive or neutral one.
Example: "I'm bad at public speaking" becomes "I can improve my public speaking with practice."

By regularly practicing these cognitive restructuring techniques, you can break free from limiting beliefs, shift your thought patterns towards more constructive perspectives, and cultivate a more positive mindset. It takes time and consistency, but with practice, these exercises can bring lasting positive change to your mental and emotional well-being.

6. **Generating Alternative Thoughts**:
After identifying a negative automatic thought, generate alternative, more balanced thoughts to replace it. Ask yourself: What's a more realistic or helpful way to view this situation? How would I advise a friend in a similar scenario? Write down these alternative thoughts and refer to them whenever negative thinking arises.
Exercise: Take a negative thought and brainstorm as many alternative, balanced thoughts as possible.
Example: "I'm worthless." Alternative thoughts: "I have strengths and qualities," "Everyone makes mistakes," "This is an opportunity to learn and grow."

7. **Using Affirmations**:
Create positive affirmations or self-statements to counteract negative thoughts and reinforce your worth and capabilities. Repeat these affirmations regularly to reprogram your subconscious mind.
Exercise: Choose an affirmation that resonates with you and repeat it daily.
Example: Replace "Nobody likes me" with "I am worthy of love and connection."

8 **Reality Testing**:
Test the accuracy of negative thoughts by gathering objective evidence or seeking feedback from others. Ask friends or family members for their perspective, and consider whether your interpretation is fact-based or an assumption.
Exercise: Pick a negative thought and seek feedback from trusted people.
Example: If you think "Nobody cares about me," ask friends how they feel about your relationship with them.

9 **Behavioral Experiments**:
Conduct behavioral experiments to challenge negative predictions. Engage in activities that counter your negative thoughts and observe the outcomes.
Exercise: Design and carry out an experiment that challenges your belief.
Example: If you think "I'll embarrass myself in meetings," challenge this by speaking up in a meeting and observe the reactions.

10 **Gratitude Practice**:
Cultivate gratitude by focusing on the positive aspects of your life. Keeping a gratitude journal can shift your focus from negativity to positivity.
Exercise: Write down three things you're grateful for each day.
Example: "I'm grateful for the support of my friends," "I'm grateful for the sunny weather," "I'm grateful for a restful night's sleep."

11 **Mindfulness Meditation**:
Practice mindfulness meditation to observe your thoughts without judgment. This practice allows you to develop a more detached and compassionate perspective on negative thoughts.
Exercise: Spend a few minutes each day in mindfulness meditation, observing your thoughts without reacting.
Example: When a negative thought arises, acknowledge it without judgment, and let it pass without becoming attached to it.

By consistently practicing these cognitive restructuring exercises, you can gradually reshape your thought patterns, foster emotional adaptability, and enhance your overall well-being. Cognitive restructuring takes practice and persistence, so be kind to yourself as you work on cultivating a more adaptive and positive mindset.

Creating Positive Affirmations: Harnessing Self-Validation for Personal Growth

Positive affirmations are powerful tools that help cultivate self-confidence, resilience, and a positive mindset. By repeating affirming statements about ourselves and our lives, we can reprogram our subconscious mind, counter negative self-talk, and embrace a more optimistic perspective. In this guide, we will explore how to craft and use affirmations effectively to foster personal growth and transformation.

Understanding Affirmations

Affirmations are positive, declarative statements that assert a desired belief or outcome. They are designed to combat limiting beliefs, self-doubt, and negative thinking by replacing them with empowering, constructive thoughts. Affirmations can address various aspects of life, such as self-esteem, health, relationships, or personal goals.

The Power of Self-Validation

Self-validation is the practice of acknowledging our own worth, strengths, and accomplishments, as well as accepting our flaws. It lays the foundation for self-esteem and personal growth, reinforcing that we are deserving of love, success, and happiness. Self-validation gives us the confidence to face life's challenges from a place of inner strength.

Guidelines for Crafting Effective Affirmations

1. **Be Positive**: Use positive language, focusing on what you want to create, rather than what you wish to eliminate. For instance, instead of "I am not afraid of failure," say, "I embrace challenges and grow through my experiences."
2. **Use Present Tense**: Frame affirmations in the present, as though the desired outcome is already happening. This reinforces the belief that your goals are within reach. Say, "I

am confident and capable," not "I will be confident and capable."

3. **Be Specific**: The more specific the affirmation, the more actionable it becomes. For example, "I am attracting prosperity and abundance" is more focused than "I am lucky."

4. **Make Them Personal**: Tailor affirmations to your unique aspirations and values. Personalized affirmations resonate more deeply with your subconscious mind. For example, "I am worthy of love and happiness" feels more authentic than "People like me."

5. **Keep Them Realistic**: While affirmations should aim high, they must also feel attainable. Avoid affirmations that may trigger doubt or resistance. Choose statements that align with your beliefs and feel achievable.

6. **Use Emotional Language**: Infuse affirmations with positive emotions such as gratitude, joy, or empowerment. For example, "I am overflowing with gratitude for the opportunities in my life" is more effective than "I have opportunities."

7. **Repeat Consistently**: Repetition is key. Incorporate affirmations into your daily routine, repeating them consistently to rewire your thought patterns over time.

Sample Affirmations for Different Areas of Life

1. **Self-Esteem and Confidence**
   o "I believe in my abilities and trust myself."
   o "I am deserving of love, respect, and happiness."
   o "I radiate confidence in everything I do."

2. **Health and Well-being**
   o "I nurture my body with care and love."
   o "I am grateful for my body's strength and vitality."
   o "I am in perfect harmony with my body, mind, and spirit."

3. **Relationships and Connection**
   o "I attract loving, supportive relationships into my life."
   o "I communicate openly and authentically with others."
   o "I am worthy of healthy, fulfilling relationships."

4. **Success and Abundance**
   o "I am capable of achieving my goals and realizing my dreams."
   o "Abundance flows effortlessly into my life."

o   "I am grateful for the opportunities that surround me."
5. **Personal Growth and Empowerment**
    o   "I embrace change and growth with enthusiasm."
    o   "I trust my intuition and wisdom to guide me."
    o   "I create a life of purpose, passion, and fulfillment."

Incorporating Affirmations into Your Routine

1. **Morning Ritual**: Start each day by repeating affirmations to set a positive tone.
2. **Visual Reminders**: Place affirmations around your home where you'll frequently see them.
3. **Affirmation Meditation**: Pair affirmations with visualization in a meditative state.
4. **Affirmation Journaling**: Write affirmations in a journal and reflect on their meaning.
5. **Bedtime Practice**: End your day with affirmations to reinforce positive thoughts before sleep.

Overcoming Resistance and Doubt

It's natural to face skepticism when starting an affirmation practice, especially if you've been accustomed to negative thinking. Here's how to navigate resistance:

1. **Start Small**: Begin with affirmations that feel comfortable and believable, then expand.
2. **Challenge Negative Thoughts**: Counter resistance with your affirmations and remind yourself of their logic and truth.
3. **Stay Consistent**: Keep practicing, trusting that consistency will bring results over time.
4. **Seek Support**: Share your affirmation journey with friends or a therapist who can provide encouragement.
5. **Track Progress**: Monitor changes in your mindset and behavior, celebrating small victories.

Positive affirmations are powerful tools for rewiring your thought patterns and shaping your reality. By crafting affirmations that resonate with your values and aspirations and using them consistently, you can foster personal growth, self-confidence, and a positive mindset. Trust in your ability to create a life filled with love, abundance, and fulfillment, and embrace the journey of self-discovery that affirmations offer. Remember, you are worthy of all the success and joy life has to offer.

Setting Boundaries: Establishing Healthy Limits for Self-Care and Respect

Setting boundaries is essential for maintaining healthy relationships, safeguarding personal well-being, and promoting mutual respect. Boundaries define the limits of acceptable behavior, establish clear expectations, and protect individuals from being overwhelmed or taken advantage of. In this comprehensive guide, we'll explore the importance of setting boundaries, practical strategies for establishing them, and tips for maintaining boundaries in various areas of life.

Understanding Boundaries

Boundaries are the physical, emotional, and psychological limits that distinguish personal space from others. They guide interactions, indicate acceptable behavior, and help individuals protect their time, energy, and resources. Though flexible, boundaries are crucial for fostering healthy relationships and practicing self-care.

Types of Boundaries

1. **Physical Boundaries**: Relate to personal space and physical touch, defining comfort levels regarding proximity and contact.
2. **Emotional Boundaries**: Safeguard feelings, thoughts, and values by ensuring individuals honor their emotions and don't take responsibility for others' feelings.
3. **Time Boundaries**: Involve how one allocates time and energy, ensuring time for rest, self-care, and avoiding over-commitment.
4. **Material Boundaries**: Set limits around possessions, finances, and resources, clarifying boundaries on lending, sharing, and protecting personal items.

The Importance of Setting Boundaries

1. **Protecting Well-Being**: Boundaries prevent others from crossing personal limits, ensuring physical, emotional, and mental health is maintained.

2. **Promoting Self-Respect**: They demonstrate self-worth and communicate that individual needs and limits are valuable.
3. **Enhancing Relationships**: Clear boundaries prevent misunderstandings and promote respect, creating healthier and more respectful relationships.
4. **Empowerment**: Boundaries empower individuals to prioritize their needs, make informed decisions, and take charge of their lives.

Strategies for Establishing Boundaries

1. **Identify Your Needs and Values**: Reflect on your personal needs, values, and limits. Clarifying these areas helps you understand what you are willing to accept in your relationships.
2. **Communicate Assertively**: Use "I" statements to express your boundaries clearly and assertively without blaming others. For example, "I need time to recharge after work, so I won't be available for phone calls after 8 PM."
3. **Be Specific and Consistent**: Define your boundaries clearly and apply them consistently to avoid sending mixed messages. Be firm about maintaining your boundaries.
4. **Set Consequences**: Establish clear consequences if boundaries are crossed, and communicate them respectfully. For example, "If this continues, I will need to step back from this relationship."
5. **Prioritize Self-Care**: Make self-care a priority by setting aside time for activities that nurture your well-being, such as relaxation or hobbies.
6. **Seek Support**: Surround yourself with people who respect your boundaries. Seek advice from friends, family, or a therapist if you need help setting or enforcing boundaries.

Maintaining Boundaries in Different Areas of Life

- **Personal Relationships**: Establish boundaries around communication, space, and emotional intimacy. Be clear with partners, family, and friends about your expectations and limits.
- **Workplace**: Set boundaries regarding work hours, workload, and professional behavior. Advocate for yourself by

managing overtime, delegating tasks, and addressing inappropriate demands from colleagues or supervisors.

- **Social Settings**: Be selective about social commitments. Learn to say no to invitations or obligations that don't align with your values or goals.

Overcoming Challenges and Resistance

Setting boundaries can be difficult, especially if you fear conflict or rejection. Here are tips for overcoming these challenges:

1. **Practice Self-Awareness**: Tune into your emotions to recognize when your boundaries are being crossed, and respond accordingly.
2. **Challenge Limiting Beliefs**: Let go of fears that setting boundaries will make you seem selfish. Understand that prioritizing your well-being is healthy.
3. **Start Small**: Begin by setting simple boundaries in low-stakes situations. Build confidence by gradually asserting more significant boundaries.
4. **Seek Support**: Get encouragement from people who understand and respect your boundaries.

Setting boundaries is a critical skill for self-care, promoting mutual respect, and fostering healthy relationships. By identifying your values, communicating assertively, and practicing self-care, you can maintain boundaries that protect your well-being and enhance your connections. With ongoing self-awareness and practice, you can live a more empowered, balanced, and fulfilling life.

Building Trust: The Foundation of Healthy Relationships

Trust is the cornerstone of strong, healthy relationships, whether personal or professional. It serves as the foundation for emotional intimacy, effective communication, and mutual respect. In this guide, we'll explore the importance of trust, strategies for building trust in relationships, and how to rebuild trust when it's broken.

1. Understanding Trust

Trust is the confidence that someone is reliable, honest, and dependable. It involves having faith in another person's intentions, integrity, and commitment to fulfilling their promises. Trust is crucial for creating a safe environment where emotional connection, vulnerability, and collaboration can thrive.

2. The Importance of Trust

Trust is essential for several reasons:

- **Emotional Connection**: Trust allows for emotional intimacy and deeper connections. When we trust, we feel secure in sharing our thoughts, feelings, and vulnerabilities.
- **Effective Communication**: Trust promotes honest communication, helping people express themselves freely without fear of judgment or rejection.
- **Conflict Resolution**: Trust helps manage conflicts constructively, knowing that both parties are committed to understanding each other and finding solutions.
- **Reliability and Consistency**: Trust grows when people consistently demonstrate honesty, integrity, and follow-through, reinforcing reliability over time.

3. Cultivating Trust in Relationships

Building trust requires intentional effort. Here are some strategies:

- **Be Honest and Transparent**: Communicate openly, share your true thoughts and feelings, and avoid withholding information. Transparency fosters a strong sense of trust.
- **Follow Through on Commitments**: Honor your promises, no matter how small. Reliable actions build trust over time.
- **Show Empathy and Understanding**: Actively listen to others, validate their emotions, and demonstrate care for their well-being.
- **Respect Boundaries**: Honor personal boundaries and space. Respecting these limits creates a sense of safety and autonomy.
- **Apologize and Make Amends**: When mistakes happen, own them. Offer sincere apologies and work to repair any harm caused, showing humility and a commitment to the relationship.

4. Rebuilding Trust

When trust is broken, rebuilding it takes time and effort. Here are steps for restoring trust:

- **Acknowledge the Breach**: Take responsibility for your actions and express genuine remorse.
- **Communicate Openly**: Discuss the issue honestly and listen to each other's perspectives. Transparency is key to moving forward.
- **Set Boundaries and Expectations**: Clearly define how to prevent future breaches and commit to respecting these boundaries.
- **Demonstrate Consistency**: Rebuilding trust requires consistent trustworthy behavior over time. Patience is essential as both parties heal and rebuild confidence.
- **Seek Support**: If needed, involve a therapist or counselor to guide the trust-rebuilding process and facilitate healthy communication.

5. Trust-Building Activities

- **Trust Falls**: In this classic exercise, one person falls backward, trusting the other to catch them. It's a practical way to demonstrate vulnerability and trust.
- **Shared Experiences**: Engage in activities that require teamwork and cooperation, such as volunteering or tackling a project together.
- **Vulnerability Exercises**: Share personal experiences or feelings in a safe space. This builds emotional intimacy and deepens trust.

Trust is the bedrock of fulfilling relationships, paving the way for emotional intimacy, effective communication, and mutual respect. Cultivating trust requires honesty, consistency, empathy, and respect. When trust is damaged, it can be rebuilt with patience and commitment. Nurturing trust in all relationships helps create resilient, healthy, and meaningful connections. Remember, trust is earned through genuine actions and should be treated as a precious element of any relationship.

Key Takeaways:

- **Understanding Internal Narratives:** This chapter delves into internal narratives, also known as self-talk, and how they significantly influence emotions, behaviors, and relationships. It provides insights into how these narratives shape one's view of themselves, others, and their environment.
- **Identifying Limiting Beliefs:** A critical step in reshaping internal narratives is recognizing limiting beliefs that fuel negative self-talk and emotional turmoil. Readers will learn how to detect recurring patterns of thoughts such as self-doubt, fear of rejection, or critical inner dialogue.
- **Challenging Negative Self-Talk:** This section introduces cognitive-behavioral strategies to challenge negative internal dialogue. Readers will explore how to question the truth behind their thoughts, replace negativity with balanced, empowering beliefs, and nurture self-compassion.
- **Cultivating Positive Affirmations:** Positive affirmations serve as an essential tool for transforming self-narratives. Readers will discover how to craft personalized affirmations that emphasize their strengths and values, incorporating these into daily practice to foster a healthier mindset.
- **Practicing Self-Compassion:** Emphasizing self-compassion, the chapter provides techniques like self-kindness, mindfulness, and recognizing shared human experiences, all of which help individuals build a more nurturing relationship with themselves.
- **Reframing Past Experiences:** Past traumas and experiences often reinforce negative self-talk. This section explores therapeutic techniques, such as narrative therapy and trauma processing, helping readers reframe past events to foster healing and resilience.
- **Creating Empowering Stories:** The ultimate goal of rewriting internal narratives is to create empowering, growth-oriented stories. Readers will learn to craft personal narratives that reflect their strengths, resilience, and capacity for positive change, leading to greater well-being and stronger relationships.

Action Steps/Call to Action:

- **Reflect on your internal narratives** and identify recurring themes or patterns of negative self-talk.

- **Practice challenging negative self-talk** and reframing limiting beliefs using cognitive-behavioral techniques and positive affirmations.

Stay engaged for the next chapter, where we will explore practical exercises and strategies for **rewriting internal narratives** and fostering greater **self-esteem, resilience,** and **well-being** in your relationships and life.

Chapter 11:
Fostering Secure Attachment in Parenting

Inter-generational patterns refer to the behaviors, beliefs, and dynamics passed down through families from one generation to the next. These patterns can shape a person's identity, relationships, and overall life experiences in both positive and negative ways. Breaking these cycles involves identifying and addressing harmful patterns while fostering adaptability, healing, and growth. In this section, we will explore the impact of inter-generational patterns, recurring themes that sustain them, and practical strategies for breaking free from their influence.

Breaking Inter-generational Patterns: Healing Generational Wounds and Cultivating Adaptability

1. *Understanding Inter-generational Patterns*: Inter-generational patterns stem from family dynamics, cultural influences, and historical experiences, influencing behaviors, communication, relationships, and belief systems. While some patterns may foster resilience and support, others perpetuate cycles of dysfunction, trauma, and adversity.
2. *Common Themes in Inter-generational Patterns*: Several recurring themes contribute to perpetuating these cycles:

- **Unresolved trauma**: Trauma such as abuse, neglect, or violence can impact emotional well-being and continue across generations.
- **Dysfunctional coping mechanisms**: Maladaptive behaviors like addiction or avoidance often become learned ways to handle stress or adversity.
- **Communication patterns**: Styles such as avoidance or conflict may limit emotional expression and connection.
- **Relationship dynamics**: Codependency or emotional distance can disrupt people's ability to form healthy relationships.

- **Cultural influences**: Cultural beliefs about family roles and social expectations can also reinforce generational patterns.

3. *Recognizing Harmful Patterns*: Awareness is the first step to breaking these cycles. Signs include:

- Repeating relationship conflicts or dynamics from past generations.
- Engaging in harmful behaviors modeled by family members.
- Feeling constrained by family expectations or unresolved emotions.
- Noticing patterns of dysfunction or instability within the family.

4. *Strategies for Breaking Inter-generational Patterns*: Intentional self-reflection and effort are necessary to disrupt harmful cycles. Consider these strategies:

- **Cultivate self-awareness**: Reflect on your family's history and its impact on your beliefs and behaviors.
- **Seek support**: Reach out to trusted people or professionals for guidance, validation, and healing tools.
- **Challenge limiting beliefs**: Replace negative beliefs with empowering ones that promote growth and well-being.
- **Practice self-care**: Prioritize emotional, physical, and mental health through mindfulness, setting boundaries, and engaging in activities that bring you joy.
- **Break the silence**: Encourage open communication around family secrets or unresolved issues.
- **Create new traditions**: Establish new customs and ways of relating that align with your values and aspirations.
- **Set boundaries**: Establish clear limits to protect your well-being, and respectfully enforce them when needed.

5. *Embracing Adaptability and Healing*: The journey of breaking inter-generational patterns requires adaptability, self-compassion, and the courage to challenge old habits. Celebrate your progress, honor your strengths, and embrace healing as a continuous process that leads to greater freedom and well-being.

Breaking inter-generational patterns is an empowering path toward self-liberation. By nurturing awareness, seeking support, and fostering open communication, you can release the influence of negative family cycles, creating healthier relationships and a more authentic life.

Fostering Secure Attachment with Children: Nurturing Emotional Bonds for Lifelong Resilience

1. **Understanding Secure Attachment**: Secure attachment refers to the deep emotional bond between a child and their primary caregiver, typically formed during early childhood. It is built on trust, consistent responsiveness, and emotional attunement from the caregiver. This secure foundation allows children to feel safe, explore their environment confidently, express emotions, and develop a positive self-image.
2. **The Importance of Secure Attachment**: Secure attachment is crucial for multiple aspects of children's development, including:
   o **Emotional regulation**: Securely attached children are better able to manage challenging emotions such as stress and anxiety, using their caregivers for comfort and reassurance.
   o **Social competence**: Secure attachment promotes empathy, cooperation, and communication, which are critical for building healthy social relationships.
   o **Cognitive development**: Securely attached children are more likely to explore and engage with their surroundings, fueling their curiosity and enhancing cognitive development.
   o **Adaptability**: Secure attachment fosters resilience by providing emotional support that helps children cope with stress and adversity more effectively.
3. **Strategies for Promoting Secure Attachment**: To nurture secure attachment, parents can create a supportive, responsive caregiving environment. Practical approaches include:
   o **Respond promptly to needs**: Tune in to your child's cues and respond consistently to their physical and emotional needs, providing comfort and care.

- Establish routines: Predictable routines like bedtime and mealtimes offer children a sense of security and stability.
- Engage in positive interactions: Spend quality time bonding through activities such as playing, reading, and singing.
- Provide emotional support: Validate your child's feelings, offer reassurance during distress, and teach them how to express emotions in healthy ways.
- Encourage independence: Support your child's exploration of their environment while providing a secure base to return to for reassurance.
- Be consistent: Maintain clear, predictable expectations and boundaries, reinforcing a stable environment that helps your child feel secure.
- Reflective parenting: Practice self-awareness as a parent, recognizing how your emotions and experiences impact your child and your caregiving approach.
4. **Building Adaptability through Secure Attachment**: Secure attachment fosters resilience and adaptability in children by providing them with the emotional tools needed to cope with life's challenges:
    - Emotional resilience: Securely attached children are more comfortable expressing their emotions, which aids in the development of healthy coping mechanisms.
    - Problem-solving skills: By feeling supported, children learn to seek help when needed and explore solutions to challenges.
    - Self-confidence: Secure attachment builds a strong sense of self-worth, helping children persevere and navigate setbacks with confidence.
    - Social support: Children with secure attachment are better able to form strong social bonds and support networks, essential for resilience.
5. **Nurturing Attachment Across Developmental Stages**: As children grow, their attachment needs evolve:
    - Infancy: Focus on meeting your baby's needs for comfort, security, and affection through responsive caregiving.

- **Toddlerhood**: Encourage exploration while providing reassurance and support as your toddler navigates new experiences.
- **Early childhood**: Continue fostering attachment through positive interactions, consistent routines, and shared bonding experiences.
- **Middle childhood**: Provide emotional support and guidance as children face new social and academic challenges.
- **Adolescence**: Balance respect for independence with availability for emotional support and mentorship during the teenage years.

Secure attachment is a fundamental element of parenting that sets the stage for a child's emotional, social, and academic success. By fostering emotional bonds through consistent care, emotional attunement, and positive interaction, caregivers can build a foundation that helps children thrive, fostering lifelong resilience and adaptability. Through this nurturing process, children are empowered to navigate life's challenges with confidence, secure in the knowledge that they are supported and loved.

Parenting Strategies for Anxious Parents: Nurturing Confidence and Resilience in Children

Parenting can be particularly challenging for anxious parents, as they may struggle with their own fears and worries. However, it's possible for anxious parents to foster confidence and adaptability in their children by implementing strategies that promote emotional well-being and security. This section explores how anxious parents can manage parenting with confidence, support their children's emotional growth, and nurture adaptability even in the face of anxiety.

1. **Understanding Parental Anxiety**: Parental anxiety often arises from concerns about children's safety, well-being, and future. It can be fueled by past experiences, societal expectations, or self-doubt about parenting abilities. While occasional anxiety is natural, chronic or excessive anxiety can hinder effective parenting and impact children's emotional development.

2. **Impact of Parental Anxiety on Children**: Parental anxiety can affect children in various ways, including:
    o **Modeling behavior**: Children tend to mirror their parents' reactions to stress, learning to perceive the world as threatening or unsafe if anxiety is prominent in the household.
    o **Over-protection**: Anxious parents may become overly protective, limiting their children's independence and hindering their ability to develop resilience and problem-solving skills.
    o **Communication challenges**: Anxiety can hinder open communication, leading to misunderstandings and difficulty expressing emotions within the family.
    o **Emotional regulation**: Anxious parents may struggle with their own emotional regulation, creating a tense or unpredictable home environment that can impact children's sense of security.
3. **Parenting Strategies for Anxious Parents**: To foster emotional well-being and adaptability in children, anxious parents can adopt the following strategies:
    o **Practice self-awareness**: Reflect on how your anxiety impacts your parenting behavior. Identifying anxiety triggers and coping mechanisms helps manage the effects of anxiety on parenting.
    o **Seek support**: Reach out to friends, family, or professionals for guidance in managing anxiety. Therapy, support groups, or parenting workshops can provide tools for effective coping and parenting.
    o **Model healthy coping skills**: Demonstrate positive ways to handle stress, such as deep breathing, mindfulness, and problem-solving, showing your children how to approach challenges calmly.
    o **Foster open communication**: Create a safe environment where children feel comfortable sharing their thoughts and feelings. Active listening and validation encourage them to express themselves without fear.
    o **Offer reassurance and validation**: When your child feels anxious, acknowledge their emotions and provide comfort. Reassure them that it's normal to feel scared at times and that they are supported.

- Encourage autonomy and independence: Support your children in making decisions, taking risks, and learning from their mistakes. This helps build confidence and resilience.
- Establish routines and predictability: Consistent routines provide stability, helping children feel secure and reducing uncertainty.
- Teach problem-solving skills: Encourage your children to face challenges by brainstorming solutions and learning to resolve issues on their own.

4. Supporting Children with Anxiety: If your child experiences anxiety, there are additional ways to help:
   - Validate their feelings: Recognize their anxiety without judgment and offer reassurance.
   - Teach relaxation techniques: Help them manage anxiety by practicing deep breathing, visualization, or muscle relaxation exercises.
   - Provide gradual exposure: Support your child in facing fears gradually, offering praise for their efforts as they build confidence in confronting challenges.
   - Seek professional help if needed: If anxiety significantly impacts your child's daily life, consider seeking therapy to provide additional support and guidance.

5. Taking Care of Yourself: Prioritize your own self-care to be an effective parent. Activities such as exercise, mindfulness, hobbies, and spending time with loved ones can help reduce anxiety and support your emotional well-being.

Anxious parents can nurture confidence and adaptability in their children by practicing self-awareness, seeking support, fostering open communication, and encouraging independence. These strategies help create a nurturing, supportive environment where children can thrive, develop emotional resilience, and face life's challenges with optimism. Parenting is a journey, and the efforts you make to support your child's emotional growth are invaluable investments in their future well-being.

Key Takeaways: • Foundations of Attachment: This chapter examines the significance of attachment in parenting and its deep influence on child development. Readers will understand how secure attachment fosters emotional security, resilience, and healthy relationships throughout a child's life. • **Secure Base**: Parents serve as a secure base from which children explore the world. Readers will discover methods for building a strong attachment bond with their children through responsive caregiving, emotional availability, and consistent routines. • **Sensitive Responsiveness**: Attuned and sensitive responses are crucial for nurturing secure attachment. The chapter highlights the importance of recognizing children's needs and emotions, validating their feelings, and responding supportively to promote trust and connection. • **Emotional Regulation**: Parents play a vital role in teaching children emotional regulation. Attentive caregiving helps children manage stress, frustration, and emotions, laying a foundation for healthy emotional regulation into adulthood. • **Parenting Styles**: The chapter examines how different parenting styles affect attachment. Authoritative parenting, which blends warmth and clear boundaries, is shown to positively influence secure attachment and child development. • **Creating a Secure Environment**: A secure environment includes both physical safety and emotional security. Readers will learn how to create a stable, nurturing, and predictable atmosphere that fosters children's sense of autonomy and confidence. • **Healing Attachment Wounds**: For parents who experienced insecure attachment in their own upbringing, healing these wounds is crucial. The chapter offers insights into reflective parenting, inner child work, and attachment-focused interventions to help parents form secure bonds with their children.

Action Steps/Call to Action: • Reflect on how your current parenting practices affect your child's attachment security. • Practice being sensitively responsive to your child's emotional cues and needs.

Stay tuned for the next chapter, where we'll dive into practical strategies to foster secure attachment and support your child's emotional development and resilience.

Chapter 12

Therapeutic Approaches for Anxious Attachment: Individual, Couples, and Group Therapy

Therapy can be an essential tool for individuals dealing with anxious attachment, providing insight, support, and strategies for healing and personal growth. Various therapy options, such as individual therapy, couples therapy, and group therapy, offer distinct advantages for addressing the challenges of anxious attachment. This chapter explores these therapeutic approaches, key considerations when seeking the right therapist, and the benefits of therapy for those with anxious attachment:

1. **Individual Therapy**: Also known as psychotherapy or counseling, individual therapy involves private, one-on-one sessions with a therapist. In therapy for anxious attachment, the therapist works collaboratively with the client to uncover the root causes of attachment issues, address maladaptive patterns of thinking and behavior, and develop practical coping strategies. This personalized approach provides a safe, confidential environment for clients to express their feelings and thoughts while receiving targeted guidance and support tailored to their specific needs.

2. **Couples Therapy**: Couples therapy, often referred to as marriage counseling, brings both partners into therapy to address relational dynamics. For those with anxious attachment, couples therapy focuses on improving communication, building trust, and enhancing emotional intimacy within the relationship. A therapist helps couples identify behaviors linked to anxious attachment, such as jealousy, insecurity, or fear of abandonment, and provides tools to strengthen their bond. This approach fosters mutual understanding, helping couples work together to create a more secure and satisfying relationship.

3. **Group Therapy**: Group therapy consists of sessions with a small group of individuals facing similar concerns. Group therapy for anxious attachment allows participants to share experiences and challenges in a supportive community. This

setting offers validation and camaraderie, making it particularly helpful for those struggling with social anxiety or forming attachments. By engaging with others who are navigating similar issues, participants gain new perspectives, practice relationship-building skills, and receive support from both peers and the therapist, promoting healing and personal growth.

Each of these therapy options provides unique benefits for addressing anxious attachment, helping individuals move toward healthier, more secure relationships and greater emotional well-being.

Considerations for Finding the Right Therapist:

Choosing the right therapist is crucial for achieving positive therapy outcomes, especially when addressing issues related to anxious attachment. Here are key considerations to keep in mind while searching for a therapist:

- **Specialization and Expertise**: Look for a therapist with experience and training in attachment theory, anxiety disorders, and interpersonal relationships. A therapist with expertise in these areas will have a better understanding of anxious attachment and will be equipped to provide effective interventions for your specific needs.
- **Personal Fit**: It's essential to feel comfortable and have a good rapport with your therapist. Consider the therapist's communication style, personality, and overall approach to therapy. You might want to schedule an initial consultation or phone call to determine if you feel at ease and connected with the therapist's manner and methods.
- **Therapy Modality**: Different therapists use varying therapeutic approaches, such as cognitive-behavioral therapy (CBT), emotionally focused therapy (EFT), or psychodynamic therapy. Choose a therapist whose therapeutic approach aligns with your personal preferences and goals for therapy.
- **Accessibility and Logistics**: Practical considerations such as location, availability, and fees are important. Ensure the therapist's services are convenient and affordable for you, and that their schedule works with yours to allow for regular sessions.

Benefits of Therapy for Anxious Attachment:

Therapy offers numerous advantages for individuals dealing with anxious attachment, including:

- **Increased Self-Awareness**: Therapy provides a safe space to explore the emotions, beliefs, and patterns contributing to anxious attachment. This self-reflection helps people better understand their relationship dynamics and behaviors.
- **Improved Relational Skills**: Therapy aids in the development of essential skills such as effective communication, conflict resolution, and boundary-setting, all of which contribute to healthier, more balanced relationships.
- **Reduced Anxiety and Distress**: Therapeutic techniques offer practical strategies for managing anxiety symptoms, alleviating fear, insecurity, and emotional distress.
- **Enhanced Self-Esteem and Confidence**: Therapy fosters self-acceptance, builds self-esteem, and promotes a positive self-image, leading to a stronger sense of self-worth and empowerment.
- **Greater Flexibility and Resilience**: Therapy nurtures adaptability and resilience, allowing individuals to handle life's challenges with greater confidence and ease.
- **Stronger, More Secure Attachments**: Through therapy, people can shift towards more secure attachment styles, characterized by trust, emotional intimacy, and deeper connections, resulting in more fulfilling relationships.

Therapy serves as a powerful tool for those grappling with anxious attachment, offering personalized support and strategies for healing and growth. Whether through individual, couples, or group therapy, individuals can work toward overcoming anxious attachment patterns and fostering more secure, satisfying relationships. With the right therapist and a commitment to the process, individuals embark on a transformative journey of self-discovery, emotional healing, and growth.

Key Takeaways:

- **Individual Therapy**: Individual therapy offers a safe, supportive environment for those with anxious attachment to explore underlying emotions and behaviors. It helps individuals gain insight into their attachment styles, process past experiences, and develop effective coping strategies for managing anxiety in relationships.

- **Couples Therapy**: Couples therapy allows partners to address relational dynamics that contribute to anxious attachment. It promotes open communication, emotional intimacy, and trust, helping couples identify negative patterns, improve conflict resolution, and build a more secure relationship.
- **Group Therapy**: Group therapy offers validation and connection with others who share similar experiences. It reduces feelings of isolation, encourages peer support, and provides opportunities for individuals to practice new skills and receive feedback within a supportive community.
- **Attachment-Focused Approaches**: Therapists may utilize techniques like Emotionally Focused Therapy (EFT) or Attachment-Based Family Therapy (ABFT) to help individuals and couples understand the emotions driving their attachment behaviors and heal attachment wounds.
- **Mindfulness and Self-Compassion**: Mindfulness and self-compassion practices are often integrated into therapy to promote emotional regulation and self-awareness. Techniques like meditation and body scans help individuals stay present, while self-compassion nurtures kindness and acceptance toward themselves and others.
- **Holistic Approaches**: Complementary practices such as yoga, meditation, and art therapy support the healing of anxious attachment by addressing the mind-body connection. These holistic approaches enhance emotional regulation, reduce stress, and foster resilience.

Action Steps/Call to Action:

- Reflect on your therapeutic needs and consider whether individual, couples, or group therapy is right for you.
- Explore attachment-focused therapy approaches and holistic practices that resonate with you.

Stay engaged for the next chapter, where we'll dive into practical strategies and techniques for healing anxious attachment and fostering greater security and fulfillment in relationships.

Chapter 13
Healing Emotional Wounds: Processing Past Trauma

Past trauma can deeply affect emotional well-being and relationships, often leading to challenges like anxious attachment, anxiety, depression, and struggles with emotional regulation. Healing from trauma is crucial for recovery, as it helps individuals confront and resolve the lingering emotions, beliefs, and patterns that influence their present lives. In this chapter, we will examine trauma-informed therapy approaches, such as Eye Movement Desensitization and Reprocessing (EMDR), Somatic Experiencing, and other methods that support healing from trauma and enhance emotional well-being.

Understanding Past Trauma:

Past trauma refers to experiences that cause significant distress, harm, or threats to one's physical or emotional well-being. Traumatic events can range from childhood abuse and neglect to accidents, natural disasters, interpersonal violence, or the loss of a loved one. Trauma often leaves lasting effects on the brain, nervous system, and emotional regulation, which can lead to symptoms such as hypervigilance, flashbacks, nightmares, avoidance behaviors, and difficulties in managing emotions.

Trauma-Informed Therapy Approaches:

Trauma-informed therapy focuses on addressing the unique needs of individuals who have experienced trauma. These approaches emphasize safety, collaboration, and empowerment throughout the healing process. Some common trauma-informed therapies include:

- **Cognitive-Behavioral Therapy (CBT):** This approach helps individuals identify and challenge negative thoughts and beliefs related to trauma, develop coping mechanisms, and gradually face traumatic memories in a supportive environment.
- **Dialectical Behavior Therapy (DBT):** DBT integrates cognitive-behavioral techniques with mindfulness practices

to improve emotional regulation, manage distress, enhance interpersonal relationships, and foster empowerment.

- **Eye Movement Desensitization and Reprocessing (EMDR):** EMDR utilizes bilateral stimulation, such as guided eye movements, to help individuals reprocess traumatic memories, reduce distress, and integrate these experiences into their lives in a healthier way.
- **Somatic Experiencing (SE):** SE is a body-based approach aimed at releasing trauma-related tension held in the body. Through techniques like breath-work and movement exercises, individuals learn to manage bodily sensations and regulate their nervous system's response to trauma.
- **Sensorimotor Psychotherapy:** This approach integrates body-centered techniques with traditional talk therapy to address trauma symptoms. It focuses on increasing awareness of bodily sensations to promote healing and emotional regulation.

Eye Movement Desensitization and Reprocessing (EMDR):

EMDR is a structured therapy that helps individuals process and integrate traumatic experiences. During sessions, clients are guided through bilateral stimulation exercises, such as tracking a therapist's finger movements or listening to alternating sounds, while recalling distressing memories. EMDR helps reduce emotional reactivity and fosters healthier processing of traumatic memories.

Somatic Experiencing (SE):

Somatic Experiencing is a body-centered approach to trauma healing that focuses on the physical manifestations of trauma held within the body. Through mindfulness, breath-work, and movement exercises, SE helps individuals become more aware of bodily sensations and their responses to trauma triggers. This method restores balance to the nervous system, fostering a sense of safety and well-being.

Other Trauma-Informed Techniques:

In addition to EMDR and Somatic Experiencing, there are several other trauma-informed techniques that can assist in processing past trauma and fostering healing:

- **Mindfulness and Meditation:** Mindfulness practices help individuals develop present-moment awareness, acceptance, and self-compassion. These practices reduce emotional reactivity to trauma triggers and promote better emotional regulation and adaptability.
- **Art Therapy:** Art therapy provides a creative and non-verbal outlet for expressing emotions and processing trauma. It allows individuals to explore their experiences, identities, and feelings in a safe and supportive environment, fostering healing through artistic expression.
- **Yoga and Movement Therapy:** Yoga and movement-based therapies combine gentle physical movement, breath-work, and mindfulness to help individuals release tension, regulate the nervous system, and promote grounding and relaxation in the body.

Trauma-informed approaches such as EMDR, Somatic Experiencing, and other techniques offer powerful and effective tools for processing past trauma and fostering recovery and emotional well-being.

The Power of Vulnerability: Embracing Authentic Connection

Vulnerability is often misunderstood as a sign of weakness, but in truth, it is a powerful source of strength and authenticity in relationships. By embracing vulnerability, individuals can foster deeper connections, build intimacy, and move beyond the fear of rejection. In this section, we explore the importance of vulnerability, strategies for overcoming fear, and the role of authenticity in creating meaningful relationships.

Understanding Vulnerability:

Vulnerability involves allowing oneself to be fully seen and heard, despite the risks of emotional exposure or uncertainty. It takes courage to express emotions, share personal thoughts, and show up authentically. Vulnerability is the key to authentic connection, allowing people to form deeper bonds based on trust, honesty, and acceptance.

The Power of Vulnerability in Relationships:

Vulnerability plays a crucial role in building emotional intimacy and trust. When people open up to one another, they create space for empathy and validation. Vulnerability fosters stronger relationships by enabling individuals to share their fears, desires, and insecurities. It strengthens bonds by allowing people to be fully themselves, leading to more meaningful and fulfilling connections.

Overcoming Fear of Rejection:

Fear of rejection often prevents people from being vulnerable, leading them to hide their true selves. To move past this fear and embrace vulnerability:

- **Challenge negative beliefs:** Identify limiting beliefs like "I'm not enough" or "I'll be rejected if I show my true self," and replace them with positive affirmations that empower your sense of worth.
- **Practice self-compassion:** Be kind to yourself during moments of vulnerability. Accept that imperfection is part of being human and that rejection does not diminish your value.
- **Start small:** Begin by being vulnerable in low-risk situations with trusted friends or family members. Build confidence as you gradually increase your openness in more challenging settings.
- **Stay present:** Let go of past rejections and future anxieties. Focus on the present moment, appreciating each opportunity for connection and growth.

Authenticity in Relationships:

Authenticity is the foundation of healthy, trusting relationships. It involves being true to yourself, expressing your thoughts and emotions honestly, and honoring your values. In authentic relationships, people feel safe to be themselves, fostering trust, acceptance, and emotional intimacy.

Cultivating Authentic Connection:

To build authenticity in relationships:

- **Practice active listening:** Listen with empathy, curiosity, and an open heart. Validate the other person's feelings and experiences, creating a space for mutual understanding.
- **Be open and honest:** Share your feelings and thoughts sincerely. Avoid hiding behind pretenses, and embrace vulnerability as a bridge to deeper connection.
- **Set boundaries:** Clearly communicate your boundaries and needs, ensuring that both parties respect and honor each other's limits. Boundaries protect authenticity by fostering mutual respect.
- **Cultivate empathy:** Seek to understand others by putting yourself in their position. Empathy fosters trust and emotional closeness, enriching relationships.

Vulnerability, when embraced, leads to stronger, more authentic connections. By overcoming the fear of rejection, practicing self-compassion, and honoring your true self, you open the door to deeper, more meaningful relationships built on honesty and mutual respect. Vulnerability is not a weakness—it's an act of courage that invites real connection into your life.

Forgiving Yourself and Others: A Journey to Healing and Freedom

Forgiveness is a powerful act of self-compassion and liberation, allowing individuals to release anger, resentment, and pain, paving the way for greater inner peace and emotional well-being. Whether directed toward yourself or others, forgiveness offers a path to healing. In this section, we explore the process of forgiving yourself and others, letting go of negative emotions, and embracing compassion and grace.

Forgiving Yourself:

Forgiving yourself involves releasing self-blame, guilt, and regret over past actions. It requires self-compassion, acceptance, and recognizing your own humanity. Follow these steps to embark on the journey of self-forgiveness:

- **Acknowledge the mistake:** Take ownership of your actions without excessive judgment. Understand that everyone makes mistakes, and you are not defined by them.

- **Practice self-compassion:** Be kind to yourself, especially during moments of self-doubt or criticism. Remind yourself that you are deserving of love and forgiveness.
- **Make amends where possible:** If your actions affected others, sincerely apologize and take steps to correct any harm caused. Commit to learning from the experience and growing.
- **Let go of perfectionism:** Release the unrealistic expectation of perfection. Embrace your flaws and see mistakes as opportunities for growth.

Forgiving Others:

Forgiving others involves letting go of bitterness and anger toward those who have caused pain. It requires empathy and a willingness to see others' humanity, even when they've hurt you. These steps can help in forgiving others:

- **Acknowledge the hurt:** Validate the pain caused by someone's actions. Allow yourself to feel and process your emotions without suppressing them.
- **Practice empathy:** Try to understand the person's motivations, circumstances, or struggles. Recognize that their hurtful actions may stem from their own challenges or vulnerabilities.
- **Release resentment:** Let go of anger and resentment, not for their sake, but for your own peace of mind. Holding onto these emotions only deepens your suffering.
- **Set healthy boundaries:** Establish boundaries to protect yourself from further harm while maintaining your integrity. Boundaries promote self-respect and allow forgiveness without compromising your well-being.

Moving Forward with Compassion and Grace:

Forgiving yourself and others is a vital step toward emotional freedom. It is not about excusing hurtful behavior or minimizing pain, but rather freeing yourself from the negative emotions that keep you stuck in the past. Forgiveness creates space for compassion, healing, and growth, ultimately leading to greater peace, healthier relationships, and personal empowerment.

Releasing Resentment and Anger: A Path to Emotional Freedom

Releasing resentment and anger is key to emotional healing and overall well-being. Holding onto these emotions prolongs suffering and keeps us from moving forward with peace and clarity. To effectively release resentment and anger, consider these practices:

- **Express your emotions:** Find healthy ways to express what you're feeling. This might involve journaling, talking to a trusted friend or therapist, or engaging in creative outlets such as art, music, or writing. Expressing emotions allows for emotional release and aids in processing difficult feelings.
- **Practice forgiveness:** Choose to forgive both yourself and others, recognizing that forgiveness is a gift you give to yourself. Let go of the desire for revenge or justification, and embrace forgiveness as a powerful tool for inner peace and personal freedom.
- **Cultivate compassion:** Develop compassion for yourself and others by recognizing the inherent worth of each individual. Practice empathy, kindness, and understanding as you extend forgiveness, approaching the process with an open heart and a generous spirit.

Moving Forward with Compassion: Steps Toward Healing

Moving forward with compassion is about embracing forgiveness as a transformative journey of healing and growth. It involves releasing the past, being fully present, and opening yourself to new possibilities. To move forward with compassion, you can:

- **Prioritize self-care:** Focus on activities that nurture your body, mind, and spirit. Whether it's through exercise, relaxation, or pursuing your passions, engage in actions that bring joy and balance into your life.
- **Cultivate gratitude:** Focus on the lessons you've learned, the strength you've developed, and the opportunities for growth that come from forgiveness. Shift your attention to the positives in your life and relationships, fostering a mindset of gratitude and abundance.
- **Foster meaningful connections:** Surround yourself with supportive and uplifting people. Build relationships based on

empathy, respect, and mutual understanding. A strong support network can inspire and encourage your journey toward healing and forgiveness.

- **Practice mindfulness:** Stay present and fully engaged in the moment. Mindfulness allows you to experience life as it is, without judgment, fostering inner peace and adaptability. Being mindful helps you regulate emotions and stay grounded in the here and now.

Forgiveness is an act of courage and self-compassion that paves the way for healing, growth, and personal transformation. By releasing anger, embracing compassion, and practicing forgiveness, you create the space for greater peace, freedom, and well-being in your life. Cultivating forgiveness leads to deeper connections and a more meaningful, fulfilling existence, both within yourself and in your relationships with others.

Key Takeaways:

- **Understanding Trauma:** This chapter delves into the nature of trauma and its effects on emotional well-being. Readers will learn about various forms of trauma, such as childhood abuse, neglect, loss, and relational betrayal, and how these experiences can influence attachment styles and relationships.
- **Acknowledging Emotional Wounds:** The first step in healing trauma is recognizing and validating emotional wounds. Readers will be guided to identify symptoms of unresolved trauma, such as intrusive thoughts, emotional detachment, and hypervigilance, and how these can contribute to anxious attachment patterns.
- **Therapeutic Techniques:** Therapy provides a structured space for processing trauma and emotional healing. The chapter covers key therapeutic techniques, including Trauma-Focused Cognitive Behavioral Therapy (TF-CBT), Eye Movement Desensitization and Reprocessing (EMDR), and somatic experiencing, which help individuals process trauma, regulate emotions, and build resilience.
- **Inner Child Work:** Inner child work focuses on reconnecting with the wounded inner self. Readers will learn how this practice helps in healing childhood trauma by

fostering self-compassion and empathy and developing a secure internal support system.

- **Attachment-Focused Therapy:** Therapies like Attachment-Based Family Therapy (ABFT) and Emotionally Focused Therapy (EFT) address the impact of trauma on attachment and relationships. These approaches help repair attachment wounds, promote trust, and create more secure and emotionally fulfilling connections.
- **Self-Compassion and Self-Care:** Healing trauma requires practicing self-compassion and prioritizing self-care. The chapter highlights practices like mindfulness, self-kindness, and understanding common humanity as ways to build self-acceptance, ease emotional distress, and nurture resilience.
- **Community Support:** The journey of trauma recovery often involves seeking support from others. Readers are encouraged to turn to trusted individuals or support groups for empathy, validation, and encouragement along their healing journey.

Action Steps/Call to Action:

- Reflect on past traumatic experiences and how they may be influencing your emotional health and relationships.
- Consider seeking therapy or professional support to work through trauma and begin the healing process.

Chapter 14:
Cultivating Self-Worth and Authenticity

As we continue on the journey of overcoming anxious attachment and fostering emotional well-being, one crucial aspect stands at the heart of lasting change: cultivating self-worth and embracing authenticity. Our self-worth—the value we place on ourselves—shapes every aspect of our lives, from our relationships to our goals and our emotional health. Authenticity, the courage to be genuine and true to oneself, is equally vital in creating meaningful connections and living a fulfilled life. In this chapter, we'll explore the importance of self-worth and authenticity, how they intertwine with attachment styles, and practical strategies for nurturing these qualities in your daily life.

Understanding Self-Worth

Self-worth refers to the deep belief that you are inherently valuable, regardless of your achievements, appearance, or others' opinions. When rooted in anxious attachment, individuals often tie their sense of worth to external validation, approval, or the need to "earn" love. This can lead to feelings of inadequacy, insecurity, and constant fear of rejection.

Recognizing that self-worth is innate is the first step toward breaking free from the patterns of anxious attachment. By cultivating an internal sense of worth, we no longer rely on others to define our value. Instead, we anchor ourselves in self-acceptance and respect, which leads to more secure attachments and healthier relationships.

The Role of Authenticity

Authenticity is living in alignment with your true self—your values, feelings, and desires. It means showing up fully in your relationships and expressing yourself without fear of judgment or rejection. Authenticity and self-worth go hand in hand. When we believe in our own value, we feel more empowered to be authentic, and when we live authentically, we reinforce our sense of self-worth.

For individuals with anxious attachment, the fear of rejection or disapproval can make authenticity feel risky. The desire to please others or avoid conflict often leads to suppressing true feelings or masking parts of oneself. This can result in emotional exhaustion, frustration, and strained relationships, as we distance ourselves from our true identity in an effort to maintain superficial harmony.

Building Self-Worth and Authenticity

The good news is that both self-worth and authenticity can be cultivated through intentional practice and self-reflection. Here are some essential strategies for fostering these qualities:

1. Practice Self-Compassion

Self-compassion is the foundation of self-worth. It involves treating yourself with kindness, empathy, and understanding—especially during times of struggle or failure. Instead of criticizing yourself for perceived shortcomings, acknowledge that imperfections and mistakes are part of the human experience. Begin by offering yourself the same grace and compassion you would offer a loved one.

2. Challenge Negative Self-Talk

Our internal narratives play a significant role in shaping our self-worth. Pay attention to the way you speak to yourself. Are you often critical or judgmental? Do you focus on your perceived flaws rather than your strengths? Begin to challenge and reframe these negative thoughts. Replace them with affirmations that reflect your inherent worth, such as "I am enough," or "I am worthy of love and respect."

3. Embrace Vulnerability

As discussed in previous chapters, vulnerability is a powerful tool for cultivating authenticity and connection. Allow yourself to be seen for who you truly are, without the need for perfection. Share your thoughts, feelings, and fears openly with trusted people. Embracing vulnerability creates space for genuine connection and builds trust in yourself and others.

4. Set Boundaries

Setting and maintaining healthy boundaries is essential for self-worth. Boundaries protect your time, energy, and emotional well-being. They allow you to prioritize your needs while respecting the needs of others. When you set clear boundaries, you reinforce the message that you deserve respect and care. This also allows you to show up authentically in relationships without feeling overextended or resentful.

5. Engage in Self-Reflection

Take time to reflect on your values, passions, and desires. What matters most to you? What brings you joy and fulfillment? Self-reflection helps you reconnect with your true self and encourages you to make decisions that align with your authentic values. Journaling, meditation, or spending time in nature are great tools for deepening your self-awareness and exploring what authenticity means to you.

6. Celebrate Your Strengths and Achievements

Celebrate the qualities and accomplishments that make you unique. Whether big or small, take time to acknowledge your strengths and the progress you've made. By focusing on your positive attributes, you reinforce your sense of worth and cultivate a positive self-image.

7. Surround Yourself with Supportive People

The people we surround ourselves with have a profound impact on our self-worth and authenticity. Choose to spend time with individuals who uplift and support you—those who appreciate you for who you truly are, not for what you can do for them. Positive relationships create a safe space for you to grow and thrive while reinforcing your self-worth.

The Impact of Self-Worth and Authenticity on Relationships

As you cultivate self-worth and authenticity, you'll notice significant shifts in your relationships. Rather than seeking approval or validation from others, you'll approach relationships from a place of mutual respect and equality. You'll be able to express your needs and desires with clarity and confidence, fostering deeper emotional intimacy and trust. By being your authentic self, you give others permission to do the same, creating more fulfilling and harmonious connections.

Embracing the Journey of Self-Discovery

Cultivating self-worth and authenticity is not a one-time task but an ongoing journey. It requires patience, self-compassion, and dedication to personal growth. There will be moments of self-doubt or fear, but remember that each step forward is a victory in itself. Trust that the process of embracing your true self will lead to greater fulfillment, happiness, and emotional freedom.

Self-worth and authenticity are transformative forces in our lives. By recognizing our inherent value and having the courage to live authentically, we empower ourselves to create meaningful connections, experience emotional freedom, and build a life aligned with our deepest values. As you continue on your journey, embrace the challenges, celebrate the growth, and trust in your ability to cultivate a life filled with love, purpose, and joy.

Chapter 15:
Fostering Resilient Relationships

Resilience is the ability to adapt, recover, and thrive in the face of challenges and setbacks. In relationships, resilience is what allows couples, friends, and family members to navigate difficulties, maintain strong connections, and grow stronger over time. In this chapter, we'll explore the importance of resilience in relationships, strategies for cultivating resilience together, and how to overcome common obstacles that can strain relationships.

The Importance of Resilience in Relationships

Every relationship will face challenges at some point—whether it's conflict, external stressors, or personal changes. Resilience is the key to navigating these challenges without damaging the bond between partners or loved ones. It allows relationships to withstand difficulties while preserving trust, emotional intimacy, and mutual respect.

Resilient relationships are characterized by adaptability, effective communication, and a willingness to work through problems together. Instead of avoiding conflict or withdrawing when things get tough, resilient partners lean into challenges and emerge stronger as a result.

Building Resilience in Relationships

Resilience doesn't happen by accident—it requires effort and commitment from both people in the relationship. Here are some strategies to help you build resilience and create a relationship that thrives, even in difficult times:

1. Cultivate Open Communication

Effective communication is at the heart of resilient relationships. It involves actively listening to each other, expressing emotions honestly, and addressing issues openly rather than bottling them up. When communication is open, partners can better understand each other's needs, feelings, and perspectives, making it easier to navigate challenges together.

Tips for Open Communication:

- Practice active listening without interrupting or assuming.
- Use "I" statements to express your feelings and needs without blaming.
- Be mindful of your tone and body language during discussions.
- Create a safe space where both partners feel comfortable sharing their thoughts and emotions.

2. Practice Empathy and Compassion

Resilience in relationships is strengthened by empathy—the ability to understand and share the feelings of your partner. When challenges arise, practicing empathy allows you to see the situation from their perspective and respond with compassion. Empathy deepens emotional intimacy and fosters a sense of connection and safety in the relationship.

Tips for Practicing Empathy:

- Acknowledge your partner's emotions, even if you don't fully understand them.
- Ask open-ended questions to explore how they're feeling.
- Reflect back what you've heard to ensure they feel understood.
- Be patient and avoid dismissing or minimizing their feelings.

3. Embrace Conflict as a Growth Opportunity

Many people fear conflict in relationships, viewing it as a sign of weakness or failure. However, conflict is a natural part of any relationship and can be an opportunity for growth and learning. Resilient couples don't shy away from disagreements; instead, they address them constructively, using conflict to deepen their understanding of one another.

Tips for Constructive Conflict:

- Approach conflict with curiosity rather than defensiveness.

- Focus on the issue at hand, not past grievances or unrelated frustrations.
- Take breaks if emotions become too intense, and return to the conversation when you're calmer.
- Collaborate to find solutions that meet both of your needs, rather than trying to "win" the argument.

4. Foster Trust and Commitment

Trust is the foundation of any resilient relationship. It allows both partners to feel secure, knowing they can rely on each other in difficult times. Trust is built through consistent actions, honesty, and commitment to the relationship's well-being. When partners feel secure in their commitment to each other, they're better equipped to face challenges together without fear of abandonment or betrayal.

Tips for Building Trust:

- Be consistent and reliable in your actions and words.
- Follow through on commitments, both big and small.
- Be transparent about your thoughts, feelings, and intentions.
- Avoid secrecy or deception, and address any breaches of trust openly.

5. Support Each Other's Growth

Resilient relationships are those in which both partners support each other's individual growth and development. Rather than viewing personal growth as a threat to the relationship, resilient couples celebrate and encourage each other's ambitions, goals, and personal interests. This mutual support fosters a sense of partnership and shared purpose, strengthening the relationship over time.

Tips for Supporting Growth:

- Encourage your partner's goals and celebrate their achievements.
- Give each other space to pursue personal interests and hobbies.
- Be open to change and growth, both individually and as a couple.

- Use each other's strengths to support the relationship's development.

6. Practice Flexibility and Adaptability

One of the key traits of resilient relationships is flexibility. Life is full of unexpected changes, from career shifts to health issues or family transitions. Resilient couples adapt to these changes together, finding new ways to maintain connection and support despite external pressures. The ability to be flexible in your expectations and roles can make the relationship stronger, even when circumstances are difficult.

Tips for Practicing Flexibility:

- Be open to adjusting roles and responsibilities as life changes.
- Stay patient and understanding when things don't go as planned.
- Reevaluate relationship goals regularly to ensure you're both aligned.
- Focus on what's within your control, and let go of the rest.

Overcoming Common Relationship Obstacles

While building resilience in relationships is rewarding, there are common obstacles that can create tension or strain if not addressed. Here's how to navigate some of these challenges:

Dealing with External Stressors

Work, finances, family, and other external stressors can place significant strain on relationships. To prevent these pressures from damaging your bond, practice open communication about how stress is affecting you, and work together to find healthy coping mechanisms. Prioritizing time together and engaging in stress-relieving activities as a couple can help maintain emotional connection even during stressful periods.

Addressing Emotional Burnout

Emotional burnout occurs when partners feel overwhelmed by the emotional demands of the relationship, often leading to feelings of detachment or frustration. If you're experiencing burnout, it's important to take time for self-care and rejuvenation. Discuss with your partner ways to balance the emotional needs of the relationship with individual well-being. Remember that supporting each other's emotional health is a shared responsibility.

Managing Relationship Ruts

All relationships go through periods of routine or stagnation, where the excitement fades, and things feel predictable. To avoid falling into a long-term rut, inject new energy into the relationship by trying new activities together, taking trips, or revisiting shared passions. The willingness to break out of routine and rediscover joy together can reignite the connection.

Conclusion: Strengthening Your Resilient Bond

Fostering resilience in relationships requires commitment, patience, and a willingness to grow together through life's challenges. By cultivating open communication, trust, empathy, and flexibility, you build a strong foundation that can withstand the tests of time and adversity. As you continue to nurture your relationship, remember that resilience is not about avoiding difficulties, but about facing them together with strength, compassion, and unwavering support for one another.

Call to Action:

As you close this chapter, reflect on your relationship and the areas where resilience can be strengthened. Begin by applying one or two of the strategies discussed, such as enhancing communication or fostering trust. Keep in mind that building resilience is an ongoing journey, and every step you take brings you closer to a deeper, more fulfilling relationship. Embrace the opportunity to grow together, knowing that with resilience, your bond will not only survive but thrive.

Conclusion

In the end, the journey to overcoming anxious attachment has been one of reflection, growth, and transformation. Throughout this book, we've explored the nature of attachment patterns, how past experiences shape our present relationships, and how embracing vulnerability and forgiveness can lead to deeper connections and emotional well-being. We've examined the root causes of anxious attachment, recognized maladaptive behaviors, and learned how to build resilience and develop secure attachments.

Key Takeaways:

- **Understanding Attachment:** Acknowledge the influence of attachment patterns on relationships and personal well-being.
- **Recognizing Anxious Attachment:** Identify the behaviors and signs of anxious attachment and how they are linked to past experiences.
- **Rewriting Internal Narratives:** Challenge negative self-talk and replace it with empowering beliefs and stories.
- **Building Emotional Regulation Skills:** Learn effective strategies for managing emotions and fostering resilience.
- **Cultivating Secure Attachment:** Build trust, embrace vulnerability, and create deeper relationships through mindful practices.
- **Healing from Past Trauma:** Process emotional wounds, heal past trauma, and foster self-compassion and resilience.

Call to Action:

As you close this book, remember that self-awareness is the foundation of change. Take the knowledge and strategies you've learned and integrate them into your daily life. Commit to rewriting negative narratives, practicing emotional regulation, and cultivating secure attachments. Seek help when needed, and always keep in mind that healing is an ongoing journey. Embrace the opportunity to deepen your connections, strengthen your self-compassion, and live a life filled with love and fulfillment. Your path to secure attachment begins now.

Looking back on this journey, recognize the courage and strength it takes to confront your deepest fears and embark on the path of self-discovery and healing. Greater self-awareness, self-compassion, and authenticity are within reach, and they bring with them a life of deeper satisfaction and meaning. I hope you remember to be gentle with yourself, honor your progress—no matter how small—and celebrate every step you take on this journey.

Healing is not a destination, but an adventure. With every step forward, you reveal your strength and resilience. Peace, joy, and fulfillment will accompany you, and love and connection will help you grow and thrive.

-- Rose Novak

www.ingramcontent.com/pod-product-compliance
Lightning Source LLC
Chambersburg PA
CBHW071214020426
42333CB00015B/1410